FAO PLANT PRODUCTION AND PROTECTION PAPER

158

Ornamental plant propagation in the tropics

by

Carmine Damiano
Head, Propagation Department
Fruit Trees Research Institute, Rome

and

Giovanni Ferraiolo
Cooperating Scientist, Propagation Department
Fruit Trees Research Institute, Rome

Under the technical guidance and coordination of

W.O. Baudoin
Senior Officer
Horticultural Crops Group
Crop and Grassland Service
FAO Plant Production and Protection Division

2005
Published by Arrangement with the
Food and Agriculture Organization of the United Nations
by
DAYA PUBLISHING HOUSE
Delhi - 110 035
for Sale and Distribution only in South-East Asia

Food and Agriculture Organization of the United Nations

Rome, 2000

"This book was originally published by the Food and Agriculture Organization of the United Nations (FAO) as FAO Plant Production and Protection Paper No. 158."

First Indian Edition 2005

ISBN 81-7035-400-5

Published by : **Daya Publishing House**
1123/74, Deva Ram Park
Tri Nagar, Delhi - 110 035
Phone: 27383999
Fax: (011) 23244987
e-mail : dayabooks@vsni.com
website : www.dayabooks.com

Showroom : 4762-63/23, Ansari Road, Darya Ganj,
New Delhi - 110 002
Phone: 23245578, 23244987

Printed at : **Salasar Imaging Systems**
Delhi - 110 35

PRINTED IN INDIA

FOREWORD

This technical publication has been prepared in order to disseminate information on recent technologies for rapid propagation of tropical ornamental plants. In a world of increased competition, the success and viability of the new undertakings may results from the promptness in reacting to new market opportunities.

The development of ornamental plants production could reveal interesting potentials for crop diversification in the evolving liberalization of trade to the benefit of developing countries.

The paper concentrates on tissue culture which is the advanced and modern propagation technology allowing for mass cloning of selected varieties or eco-types. It is hoped that this technical paper will be instrumental to enhancing the technical capacity of public institutions and private entrepreneurs, thus leading to new production and market opportunities. It is also expected that the application of tissue culture propagation techniques will facilitate and encourage the use of ornamental plant diversity which is still largely untapped.

Floriculture is a programme area covered by the Horticultural Crops Group of the Crop and Grassland Service within the Plant Production and Protection Division. Recent trends indicate that market demand for floriculture products are expanding. Floriculture could therefore play an increasing role in horticultural development strategies for crop diversification and income and employment generation, especially for the integration of women and youth in economic activities.

We wish to acknowledge the scientific cooperation with the Fruit Trees Research Institute at Ciampino, Rome in Italy, which has enabled to compile this interesting document.

Special thanks are also extended to Ms. Barbara Horsley and Ms. Lucie Herzigova for thc cditing and formatting of the text.

Marcio Porto
Chief
Crop and Grassland Service
Plant Production and Protection Division

TABLE OF CONTENTS

LIST OF TABLES

Page

LIST OF FIGURES

LIST OF PLATES

1. INTRODUCTION

Vegetative multiplication of plants is a simple concept that can be explained as the ability of plants to reproduce themselves without any sexual process such as the fusion of gametes and the subsequent origin of a zygotic embryo. Many species, however, do not genetically possess this capacity, i.e., they multiply only through reproductive organs; others are capable of both sexual reproduction and vegetative multiplication; while a considerable number have lost the ability for the former and developed the faculty of giving rise to new individuals through specialised systems such as runnering, layering and budding.

In general, plants that have been produced without sexual reproduction show a phenotype, which is identical to that of the "mother" plant. This is one of the fundamental aspects of "cloning". In other words, whenever a plant reproduces itself vegetatively it produces a "clone". Although sexual reproduction can also create clones, vegetative multiplication, hereafter called propagation, always gives rise to cloning.

Since man has discovered that clones have identical features to those of the mother plant, many species of agronomic interest have been studied so as to enhance their natural ability to vegetatively multiplicate. The selection of the more productive plants or of those more suitable to man's needs has given birth to propagation and nurseries.

Many factors have favoured the development of the propagation industry: the advances in fundamental plant biology knowledge; the improvement of technology, and the production of synthetic hormones. These factors have permitted the propagation of the plant at specific *ex situ* sites, often very far from the original location.

The concepts expressed so far remind us that the use of soils and specific substrates and the growth of an entire plant have led to nurseries, gardens and greenhouses. In 1902, Gottlieb Haberlandt predicted that embryos could be produced from vegetative cells. Two years later E. Hanning cultured zygotic embryos excised in an immature stage from seeds, and in 1920 seedlings of orchids were germinated *in vitro*, in aseptic culture on artificial medium. It was evident that plant propagation was moving towards new approaches and technologies. However, it was only 40 years later that G. Morel and C. Martin grew dahlia shoots and potatoes from meristematic apexes. Modern *in vitro* propagation was born, later to be known as "micropropagation".

At present not only meristems, meristematic apexes and buds are used as primary explants to initiate the micropropagation process. In fact, "cell totipotency" is exploited to regenerate shoots and somatic embryos in many crops, ornamental and forestry species. Cell totipotency is the ability of a single cell to reconstruct a plant *in toto* similar to that from which it was excised.

2. THE LABORATORY

2.1 FACILITIES

Three separate areas are needed. This is due to the nature of the work itself. In fact, one area is devoted to the chemical preparation of the artificial culture media, a second is needed for the work to be carried out under sterile conditions and the third is that of the growth room, housing the sterile containers with the explants and plantlets growing under artificial light and at controlled temperatures.

When designing the laboratory it is important to ensure that each area conforms to certain basic requirements. A sterile environment is essential for the transfer chamber. Even the slightest contamination occurring during the transfer of the explants is responsible for heavy loss of material and enormous delay in plant production. On the other hand, total isolation of this sector is impossible without compromising the smooth functioning of the laboratory. This chamber should be aerated through dust-collecting air-filters and connecting hatches between the media preparation area and growth room would be advisable.

2.2 EQUIPMENT

2.2.1 Water purification

Water is one of the fundamental factors in tissue culture. Artificial media for growing *in vitro* culture require a very careful balance of nutrients, growth regulators and other components. Since the composition of the media can be altered by the impurities present in water, this must be as pure as possible. The lowest degree of purity acceptable is defined by a minimum resistivity of 200 000 ohms/cm. The following three methods are generally used to remove the chemicals naturally contained in water: distillation, deionization and reverse osmosis.

- *Distillation*: Low cost, free standing, electric stainless steel still units are normally available. These small apparata produce 4-5 litres of distilled water per hour, sufficient for a small laboratory processing one hundred jars per day. This kind of still unit is particularly recommended, as it is easy to repair and carry out maintenance work. Glass distilling units serve the same purpose and provide better quality water, but there is a very high risk of breaking the glass ampoules used for boiling.

- *Deionization* is a popular system used in those laboratories where local technicians provide assistance when mechanical problems appear. Water is passed through positive and negative ion exchange resins, where its salts are released. After the resins are exhausted (all the ions are replaced by the salts) regeneration is essential and occurs through washing with hydrochloric acid and sodium hydroxide. Use of disposable cartridges facilitates the work, but there is a proportionate increase in the cost of production of distilled water.

- *Reverse osmosis* is the diffusion of a fluid through a membrane into a higher concentrated solution. This system is rarely used to produce ready-to-use water; it is commonly adopted as a pre-still or pre-deionizer. For standard micropropagation activities and in the presence of normal water it is not needed.

2.2.2 Scales

Due to the wide range of weights involved, from a few milligrams to several grams, two types of scales are recommended: one analytical, with an accuracy of at least 0.1 milligrams, and one technical with a precision of 0.1 grams. There are several types of scales available on the market today. Care must be taken when buying the analytical scale as it will be used for the weighing of hormones and vitamins.

2.2.3 pH meters

The explants grown *in vitro* generally have a high capacity of adaptation to small pH variations in the media; however, continuous changes negatively affect the growth and the success of rooting. It is therefore recommended that a good quality pH meter be provided, equipped with self-regulating electrodes, sensitive to room temperature; a spare set of electrodes should always be available.

2.2.4 Hot plate stirrers

A minimum of four units of medium size and power (500 W) is required. They are used for dissolving chemicals, for shaking (tossing) during sterilisation of the explants and for preparing the agarised media. This latter operation can also be carried out in a steel container with a top-mounted stirring motor, heated on a gas burner.

2.2.5 Explant cleaning material, media dispenser and dishwasher

Several laboratories use sophisticated equipment, such as vacuum pumps and ultrasonic cleaners, to control the sterilising procedures of the vegetative material. Although helpful they are not essential, since most of the contamination occurs on the external layer of the tissue and can be neutralised only through direct contact with the sterilising agents. The use of a stirrer and some tensioactive in the disinfectant solution is always recommended. The explants should remain in the solution for the length of time established through the experimental trials. It is rather doubtful that a method will be discovered for the successful removal of endogenous bacteria or fungi.

The acquisition of an automatic media dispenser depends upon the size of the laboratory and on how many tubes and containers must be filled. It is not considered economically feasible for less than a thousand containers per day.

A dishwasher is recommended. Dishwashers specifically for laboratory use are very expensive and can be replaced by home dishwashers, bearing in mind that the last rinse cycle must utilise distilled water.

2.2.6 Sterilising equipment

Sterilisation of the tools and the media is one of the most delicate phases in the micropropagation laboratory. The size of the autoclave must be well proportioned to the amount of work to be done. A medium size autoclave has a cylindrical sterilising chamber with a diameter of 50 cm and a depth of 70 cm; this size allows to load 60-65 half-litre jars. With a single-wall autoclave (where steam is produced in the sterilising chamber) the duration of a cycle is about 85-100 minutes; when using a double-wall type (steam is produced in a separate pressure chamber from which it flows at the desired pressure, ready to use at any time) the cycle lasts 40-45 minutes. It is essential to use good quality autoclaves, since bad sterilisation compromises the work done during months of activity. If the laboratory is located far from the repair and maintenance centres, the use of simple operating equipment is recommended, as routine maintenance can be directly taken care of by the laboratory technicians.

2.2.7 Refrigerators

Two or three household refrigerators are useful to store perishable chemicals and stock solutions. A deep freezer is also needed to store special products or to keep them for a longer length of time. It is sometimes helpful to also have large or walk-in refrigerators to store the cultures or plantlets when they are ready for transfer to the greenhouses or nurseries.

2.2.8 Microscopes

Dissecting and compound microscopes are tools to be routinely kept in the micropropagation laboratory. The dissecting microscope is required for obtaining meristem starts and for examination of the growing explants during the first phases of growth. The compound microscope is not really essential, but it is useful when more accurate investigation is necessary, for example the identification of contamination or the examination of adventitious regeneration.

2.2.9 Transfer chamber

This is the site where the laminar flow cabinet is located. It must be a clean area, preferably with washable walls and floors. Openings to the exterior should be carefully sealed when the cabinets are working, in order to reduce the dust accumulation in the pre-filters, which must be frequently replaced to prolong the life and efficiency of the HEPA (High Efficiency Particulate Air) filters. These ensure sterility by retaining particles as small as 0.3 micron, the size of one of the smallest known microbes.

The laminar flow hood is also an important item of equipment. Although a different procedure, such as the use of still air boxes, could be adopted when creating a sterile work environment, the provision of one good quality sterile laminar flow hood is highly recommended. Its functioning is very simple: the air is forced to pass through special filters and to flow towards the operator, thus leaving the interior of the cabin free of particles. A double-seated model is recommended to enable the operator to place in the cabin a large number of containers with the explants to be transferred.

2.2.10 Growing room

This is a section of the micropropagation laboratory where the explants and plantlets growing in the test tubes are kept under artificial light, at an appropriate temperature and photoperiod.

The intensity and the quality of light and temperature control are critical factors. Fluorescent cool industrial white lights are generally required and considered sufficient; the light intensity at explant level should be around 2 500-3 000 lux. A good conditioning unit is needed to keep the temperature at 23°-26°C; the light ballast should be mounted externally so as to reduce the heat sources in the room, while limited air circulation maintains the temperature at a constant level. Accurate cleaning must be ensured: through removal of dust and cleansing of floors and surfaces with sterilising solutions. In this respect, in order to avoid the creation of resistant contaminants, it is highly recommended that different sterilising solutions be used, alternating them as often as possible.

2.3 SUPPLIES

The following list is an example of supplies needed to establish a small laboratory (about 50 000-100 000 plants per year).

Table 1 LIST OF SUPPLIES

Item	Size/Capacity	Quantity
Alcohol eth. 70%	500 ml	5
Alluminum foils	8 m	5
Beaker	100 ml	10
Beaker	250 ml	10
Beaker	500 ml	5
Beaker	1 000 ml	5
Canning jars	500 ml	500
Cotton hydrorepellent	500 g	10
Cotton wool	500 g	25
Culture tubes	25 mm diam.	1 000
Caps for culture tubes		1 000
Detergent (household)	1 litre	10
Petri dishes	15 cm diam.	100
Sodium hypo (bleach)	1 litre	10
Erlenmeyer flask	1 000 ml	10
Erlenmeyer flask	2 000 ml	10
Filter paper	40 x 60 cm	10 kg
Forceps (stainless)	20 cm	5
Forceps	10 cm	5
Forceps (fine tips)	10 cm	5
Graduated cylinders	50 ml	5
Graduated cylinders	100 ml	10
Graduated cylinders	250 ml	10
Graduated cylinders	500 ml	5
Graduated cylinders	1 000 ml	5
Knife holders	18 cm	10
Blades for knife holders		1 000
Marking pens		20
Pipets (graduated)	1 ml	20
Pipets	2 ml	20
Pipets	5 ml	20
Pipets	10 ml	20
Pipets	20 ml	20
Spatulas (diff. sizes)		10
Test tube racks (48 holes) for 25 mm		
Thermometer	0°-150°C	3
Timer (household)		4
Rinsing bottles	250 ml	5
Rinsing bottles	500 ml	10

Note: Most of the above items are made of Pyrex glass. Whenever possible, purchase of the disposable versions of the same is recommended, as they are cheaper.

3. PREPARATION OF MEDIA

3.1 THE STOCK AND MOTHER SOLUTION

Since the amount of chemicals required for the preparation of the solution is often very small and, consequently, weighing is difficult and inaccurate, it is advisable to proceed with the preparation of a stock and mother solution. Stock solutions are those in which one element only is dissolved at a high concentration; generally, for macro-elements it is 50 g per litre and for microelements from 0.1 to 1 g per litre. Macro, micro, hormones and vitamin mother solutions are those that contain all the chemical components of the formula with a concentration 10-20 times higher than that of the final solution. To prepare these mother solutions, proportional volumes from each stock solution must be mixed and adjusted to the right volume. The following is an example for the preparation of a mother solution of macro salts using the Murashige and Skoog formula.

Table 2 MOTHER SOLUTION OF MACRO SALTS USING THE MURASHIGE AND SKOOG FORMULA

Chemical	**Stock conc.** *(g/l)*	**Quantity to be taken for mother** *(ml)*	**Quantity to be taken from mother** *(ml)*	**Final conc.** *(mg/l)*
KNO_3	50	380		1 900
NH_4NO_3	50	330		1 650
$CaCl_2.2H_2O$	50	88		440
$MgSO_4.7H_2O$	50	74		370
KH_2PO_4	50	34		170
Distilled H_2O		94		
Total x 10 mother solution		1 000	100	
Distilled H_2O			900	
Total x 1 final solution			1 000	

It is not necessary to store the macro and micro solution at fridge temperature, although the following is recommended: freezing the stock solution of vitamins and hormones, keeping their mother solutions refrigerated and replacing these with freshly prepared ones every 15 days.

Below are a few recommendations to be followed when preparing the chemicals:

1) When mixing the products, follow the order given; this often avoids precipitation of compounds.
2) Gently warm the compounds whose reaction is endothermic and vice versa.
3) Prepare the x 200 mother solution of iron chelates as follows:
   - dissolve g 5.56 $FeSO_4.7H_2O$ in 300 ml distilled H_2O;
   - dissolve g 7.44 Na_2EDTA in 300 ml distilled H_2O;
   - mix both and heat to boiling point;
   - cool overnight at room temperature;
   - using distilled water, adjust volume to 1 000 ml distilled water.

4) A reasonable mother concentration for vitamins and hormone is 0.1 mg per ml. Vitamins are generally water soluble. Citokinins should first be dissolved in a few ml of 0.1 N HCl (occasionally a little heating is needed), then adjusted to the desired volume; at times it is useful to adjust the pH of the mother solution to a value of around 7 in order to avoid a rapid degradation of the hormone.

Auxin's salt is water soluble. Pure crystalline auxins are dissolved in small amounts of 99% ethanol; the volume is then adjusted. If precipitation should occur, more alcohol is to be added or, alternatively, the solution gently heated. The latter method should be adopted when a solution with high concentration is stored at fridge temperature.
Boric acid is better dissolved through gentle heating.

5) Solutions 0.1 and 1 N of sodium hydroxide and hydrochloric acid should always be ready for use for pH adjustment. Broad adjustments are made using 1 N solutions and refinement with 0.1 N.

6) Three compounds are added to the media in powder form:
- sugars (saccharose, glucose, fructose, others);
- gelling agent (agar-agar, gelrite, other agar substitutes), and
- charcoal (only when specifically required by the formula).

It is recommended that these products be added after the pH adjustment of the media and before starting to boil the solution.

3.2 Steps for media preparation

- prepare the stock solutions;
- prepare the mother solutions;
- prepare and mix the compounds of the chosen medium;
- adjust the pH to the desired value (ranges between 5.2 and 6.0);
- add sugar gelling agents and, eventually, charcoal;
- heat, while stirring, to sub-boiling point (at this temperature the agar is dissolved and the solution is almost clear);
- place in the containers (test tubes, jars or other containers resistant to 140°-150°C);
- wrap these containers in paper (keep them in an upright position!);
- sterilise in autoclave at 1 atmospherc pressure (corresponding to 121°C approx.);
- eject the steam very slowly (to avoid rapid boiling of media);
- rapidly cool the containers, and
- store the containers in the fridge in the dark.

4. ESTABLISHMENT OF ASEPTIC CULTURES

As the vegetative cells have the ability to reproduce new plants, any part of the plant can be collected as an initial explant from which new individuals will originate. However, in the micropropagation protocols, it is always desirable to start with pre-formed shoots or meristematic apexes. The reason for this is that when plants are originated through adventitious processes, the development of plants which are not true-to-type is likely to result. This is something to be absolutely avoided when cloning.

4.1 STERILISATION

The apexes of dormant and lateral buds which are 2-3 cm long must be surface-sterilised before commencing culture. It is highly recommended to collect this material from actively growing and healthy plants, since it would be almost impossible to successfully sterilise endogenously contaminated material.

Although there are many sterilising agents, the most commonly used are: alcohol 70%, calcium or sodium hypochlorite at 1% free chlorine, sodium mertiolate 0.5 % (mercuric salt). Technicians should rely on their own experience, bearing in mind that the tissues to be cultivated must not be damaged. The ideal material should have the inner meristematic apex absolutely pathogen free, and the sterilisation of the most external parts only should be required. The latter segments are removed with sterile tools (forceps, razor, etc.). Tensioactive compounds are recommended to allow the active principles to penetrate the tiniest niche. The use of antibiotics is not recommended unless under very particular circumstances (other buds not available, very rare and valuable genotypes, etc.), since there is a high risk of generating antibiotic-resistant bacteria.

4.2 EXPLANTING A MERISTEMATIC APEX

Although it is recommended that micropropagation be initiated with a meristem, as this is generally pathogen free, many species have difficulty in resuming cell division and organ formation when this part of the bud is cultivated without the first two-three leaf primordia. Therefore a meristematic apex, consisting of meristem and some primordia, is a reasonable compromise when establishing first cultures. The size of this organ varies according to species; it generally ranges between 0.1 and 0.5 mm, although in some monocots it can reach 2 mm. For this reason a good quality binocular stereomicroscope, having a good field depth, is needed during the preparation, which essentially consists of removing, under sterile conditions, all the leaves around the apex. During this operation, it is important that the tissues do not dehydrate as a result of the long exposure to the air flow of the laminar flow cabinet.

4.3 ROLE OF HORMONES IN MICROPROPAGATION

Skoog and Miller were the first authors who demonstrated the importance in the balance of the exogenous auxin/cytokinin when addressing *in vitro* organogenesis. The general effects of this balance are shown in Figure 1:

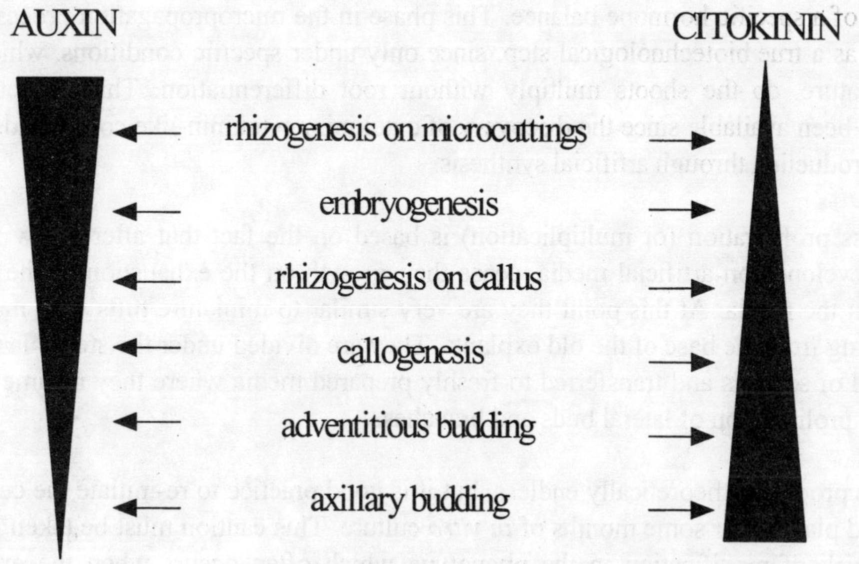

Fig. 1 CONTROLLING ORGANOGENESIS ACCORDING TO HORMONE BALANCE (from Zyrd, 1988)

However, there are some cases for which the response differs from that expected:

- Some species require a quantity of auxin added to the cytokinin in order to obtain axillary bud proliferation.
- In monocot species auxins induce strong callus proliferation.
- In monocot species organogenesis is favoured by a strong limitation of auxin after a period of cultivation under auxin control.

When employing exogenous hormones it must be borne in mind that they can have two different effects: direct modification of the cell mechanism, or influence on the balance of endogenous growing substances. More exhaustive information on the action and specific role of growing substances used in micropropagation can be found in Zyrd (1988) and George and Sherringhton (1990).

5. MASS PROLIFERATION

This covers all those procedures which allow the multiplication of axillary buds under the control of a specific hormone balance. This phase in the micropropagation process must be considered as a true biotechnological step, since only under specific conditions, which are not found in nature, do the shoots multiply without root differentiation. This "shoot-to-shoot" process has been available since the discovery of cytokinin, cytokinin-like compounds and their industrial production through artificial synthesis.

Mass proliferation (or multiplication) is based on the fact that after a few weeks the explants, developed on artificial media, cease their growth on the exhaustion of the chemicals contained in the media. At this point they are very similar to miniature tufts with many lateral shoots issuing from the base of the old explants. They are divided under the sterile laminar flow with the aid of scalpels and transferred to freshly prepared media where they resume the cycle, growth and proliferation of lateral buds and branches.

The process is theoretically endless, but it is good practice to re-initiate the culture from normal field plants after some months of *in vitro* culture. This caution must be taken in order to avoid the risk of modification in the phenotype which often occurs when the explants are cultivated for a long time. Although there are some experimental indications, the duration of this period is very variable and is in relation to the genetic background of the material that is being utilised.

When single cuttings have developed a good, well-connected to the stem, and functional root system, the *in vitro* phase is completed. The plants should now be transplanted for normal cultivation. Some morphological and physiological features make this propagating material very delicate and atypical. When a cross-section of the leaves is examined under a light microscope, the first observation is that the palisade tissue is largely vacuolated and the cells contain less chlorophyll than the leaves of normal seedlings. The epidermis is poorly protected by cuticula, and stomata are frequent and open.

The above condition can lead the plants to a rapid death by dehydration. Humidity must be very gradually reduced after the explants are placed in the greenhouses. Transparent plastic coverings generally tend to maintain high humidity levels and satisfactory lighting, thereby inducing chlorophyll photosynthesis to resume the normal process which was reduced *in vitro* due to the presence of carbon sources, such as sugars.

6. HARDENING

Even though rooting is perfect, roots lack the capillary absorbent system; because of this, water and nutrient transport to the plant is further delayed. Therefore, during the first days, care must be placed in the quality of the substrates; starting from a mixture of peat-moss/sand/perlite 1:1:1 in volume and a pH of 6.

Because of the weakness of the plant material, care must be taken in protecting the plants from soil and air-borne diseases. The major risks derive from those organisms which are responsible for stem and root rot. Unfortunately, they belong to different families and different strategies must be adopted in prevention and curing. Most of the rot symptoms are due to *Phytophthora* spp., *Pythium* spp., *Rhizoctonia* spp. and *Fusarium* spp. Before planting, it is always advisable to treat the soil with steam and appropriate chemicals.

It is recommended that the humidity be gradually reduced after 15-18 days. Large shaded greenhouses are equipped with tunnels or tents on benches. These enclosures are variously equipped with mist, bottom heat, exhaust fans, cooling pads or lighting with appropriate timing and sensing devices. A fog system is an ideal way of maintaining high humidity without over-saturating the plants, but the high cost and expensive maintenance of this system do not recommend it for adoption in those areas where assistance is poor.

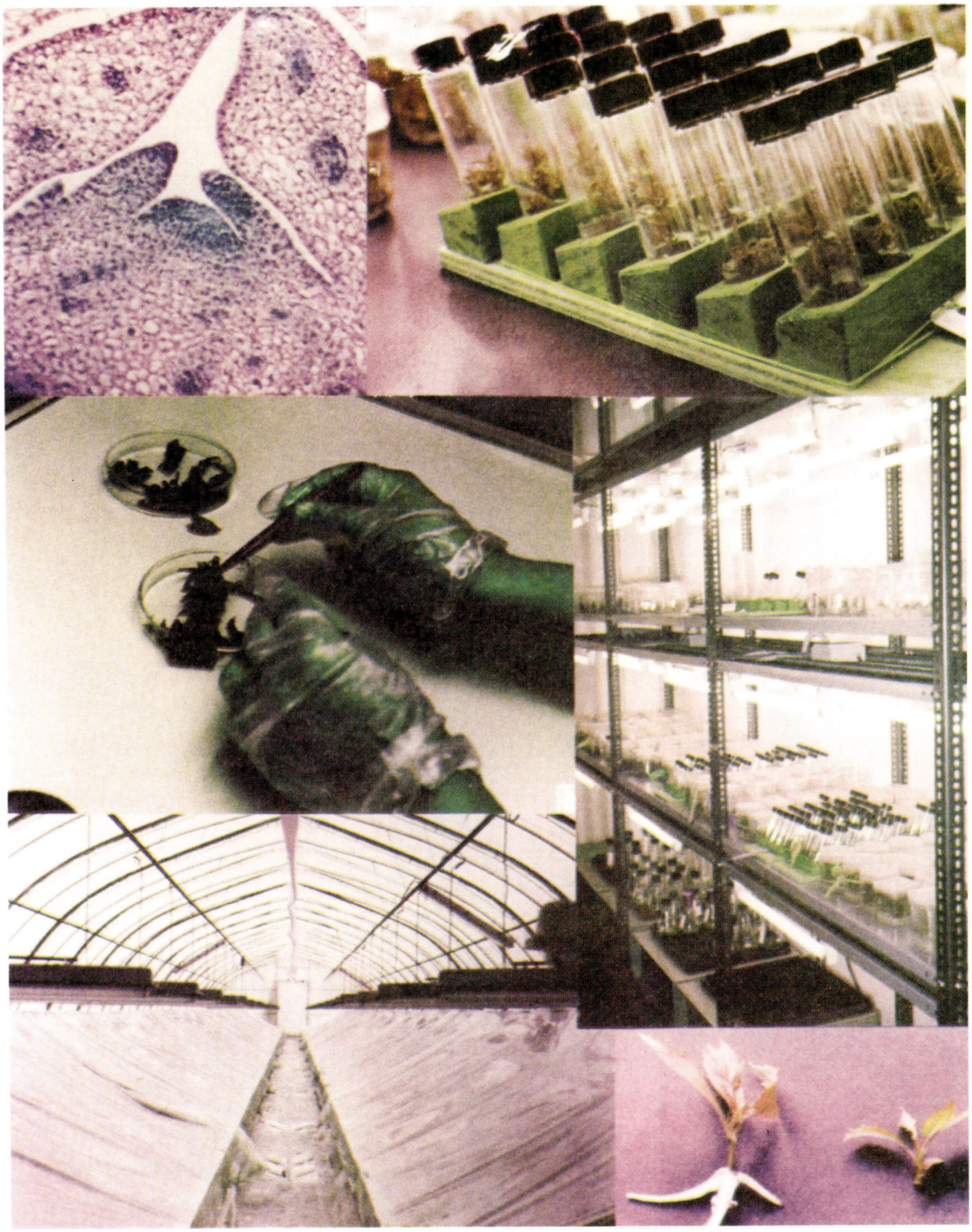

On the job (left to right, top to bottom)

Plate 7 CROSS SECTION OF MERISTEM APEX (X 25)

Plate 8 FIRST ASEPTIC ESTABLISHMENT

Plate 9 DIVISION AND TRANSFER OF EXPLANTS IN THE STERILE LAMINAR FLOW CABIN

Plate 10 GROWTH ROOM, SHELVES AND LIGHTING

Plate 11 HARDENING; HUMIDITY MAINTAINED WITH THIN PLASTIC FILM

Plate 12 ROOTED EXPLANT AT THE COMMENCEMENT OF HARDENING

At the market (top to bottom)

Plate 13 FLOWER PREPARATION AT BARBADOS FARM

Plate 14 PACKAGE FOR SHIPPING TO EXPORT MARKETS

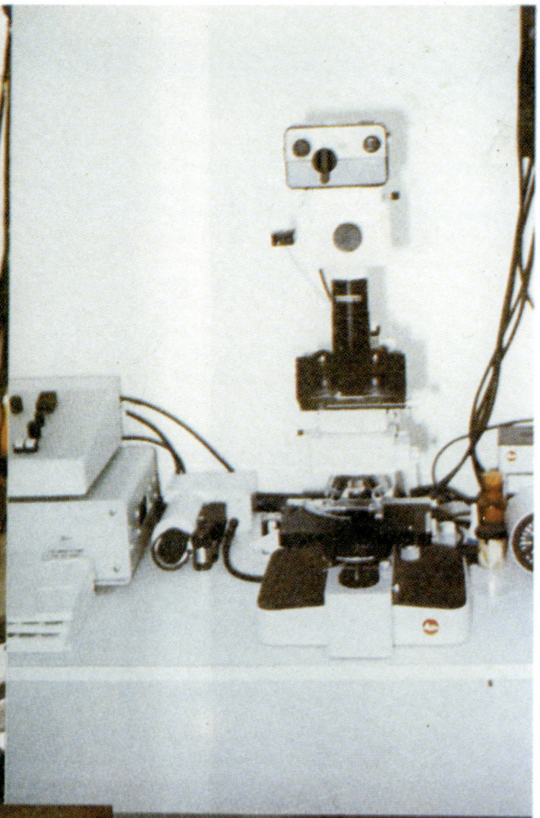
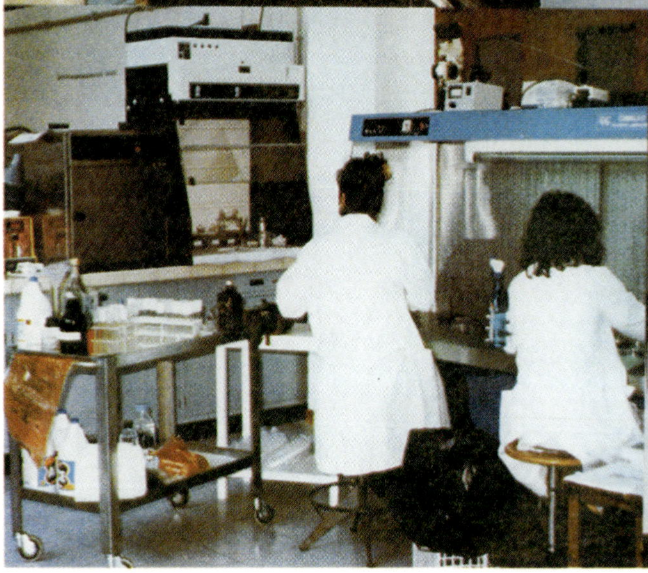

Equipment (left to right, top to bottom)

Plate 15 GROUP OF AUTOCLAVE (front), DEMINERALIZER (rear left), GLASS DISTILLING (rear right)

Plate 16 RESEARCH MICROSCOPE

Plate 17 GROUP OF LANINAR FLOW (right), INCUBATOR AND CHEMICAL HOOD

Plate 18 MICROSCOPE STEREOSCOPE

7. CASE HISTORIES

PLANT INDEX:

Botanical name	Common name	Family
Acalypha wilkesiana	Copperleaf	Euphorbiaceae
Aechmea fasciata	Aechmea	Bromeliaceae
Agapanthus umbellatus	Agapanthus	Liliaceae
Aloe barbadiensis	Aloe	Liliaceae
Alpinia pupurata	Red ginger	Zingiberaceae
Anthurium x cultorum	Anthurium hybrids	Araceae
Asclepias curassavica	Blood flower	Asclepiadaceae
Bauhinia variegata	Bahunina	Caesalpiniaceae
Bougainvillea glabra	Bougainvillea	Nyctaginaceae
Caesalpinia pulcherrima	Barbados pride	Caesalpiniaceae
Calotropis gigantea	Calotropis	Asclepiadaceae
Cassia didymobotrya	Candle bush	Caesalpiniaceae
Catharantus roseus	Madagascar periwinkle	Apocynaceae
Codiaeum variegatum	Croton	Euphorbiaceae
Cordyline fruticosa	Good-luck plant	Liliaceae
Costus speciousus	Crape ginger	Zingiberaceae
Euphorbia fulgens	Scarlet plume	Euphorbiaceae
Euphorbia pulcherrima	Poinsettia	Euphorbiaceae
Gloriosa superba	Glory lily	Liliaceae
Guzmania lingulata	Guzmania	Bromeliaceae
Heliconia psittacorum	Parrot's plantain	Musaceae
Jatropha panduraefolia	Peregrina	Euphorbiaceae
Liatris spicata	Blazing star	Compositae
Momordica charantia	Balsam pear	Cucurbitaceae
Mussaenda erytrophylla	Red flag bush	Rubiaceae
Neoregelia carolinae	Neoregelia	Bromeliaceae
Passiflora cerulea	Blue passion-flower	Passifloraceae
Plumbago indica	Plumbago	Plumbaginaceae
Strelitzia reginae	Bird of paradise flower	Musaceae
Thevetia peruviana	Yellow oleander	Apocynaceae

Botanical name: ***Acalypha wilkesiana*** Muell. Arg. 'Macrophylla'
Common name: Copperleaf

TECHNIQUES:

Bud branching from stem node segments (Stoltz, 1979)

MS medium
sucrose 20 g l^{-1}
BAP 0.2 mg l^{-1}
pH 5.8
agar 6 g l^{-1}

Rooted plantlets from shoots (Stoltz, 1979)

Macronutrients: White (1954)
Micronutrients: Stoltz (1979)
sucrose 20 g l^{-1}
pH 5.8
agar 6 g l^{-1}

REFERENCES:

Stoltz, L.P. (1979) "*In vitro* propagation of *Acalypha wilkesiana* (Copperleaf)". in. *HortScience* no. 14, p 702-703.

Botanical name: ***Aechmea fasciata*** (Lindl.) Baker

Common name: Aechmea

TECHNIQUES:

Adventitious bud induction and shoot proliferation from lateral buds (Hosoki and Asahira, 1980)

Macronutrients, amino acids and amides: MS
Micronutrients: Ringe and Nitsch (1968)
Vitamins: Nitsch and Nitsch (1965)
sucrose 20 g l^{-1}
NAA 1 mg l^{-1}
BAP 1 mg l^{-1}
agar 7 g l^{-1} (only in shoot proliferation)

Rooted plantlets from shoots (Hosoki and Asahira, 1980)

Macronutrients, amino acids and amides: MS
Micronutrients: Ringe and Nitsch (1968)
Vitamins: Nitsch and Nitsch (1965)
sucrose 20 g l^{-1}
NAA 0.1 mg l^{-1}
agar 7 g l^{-1}

REFERENCES:

Hosoki, T. and T. Asahira (1980) "*In vitro* propagation of Bromeliads in liquid culture" in *HortScience* no. 15, p 603-604.

Other references:

Jones, J.B. and T. Murashige (1974) "Tissue culture propagation of *Aechmea fasciata* Baker and other bromeliads" in *Comb. Proc. Int. Plant Prop. Soc.* no. 24, p 117-126.

Zimmer, K. and W. Pieper (1976) "Methods and problems of clonal propagation of bromeliads *in vitro*" in *Acta Horticolturae* no. 64, p 25-29.

Ziv, M., T. Yogev and O. Krebs (1986) "Effects of paclobutrazol and chlormequat on growth pattern and shoot proliferation of normal and variant *Aechmea fasciata* Baker plants regenerated *in vitro*" in *Israel Journal of Botany* 35, nos 3-4, p 175-182.

Botanical name: ***Agapanthus umbellatus*** L'Hér.
Common name: Agapanthus

TECHNIQUES:

Shoot proliferation and rooted plantlet from apical shoot (Apollonio *et al.*, 1989)

- Small callus and unique shoot (rooted shoot on the same medium)

MS medium
sucrose 35 g l^{-1}
IAA (or NAA) 1-5 mg l^{-1}
KIN 1 mg l^{-1}
pH 5.8
agar 10 g l^{-1}

- Large callus and multiple shoots

MS medium
sucrose 35 g l^{-1}
IAA (or NAA) 1-5 mg l^{-1}
BAP 10 mg l^{-1}
pH 5.8
agar 10 g l^{-1}

(shoots produced will root on the following medium)
MS medium
sucrose 35 g l^{-1}
IBA 10 mg l^{-1}
pH 5.8
agar 10 g l^{-1}

REFERENCES:

Apollonio, G., F. Scaramuzzi and S. D'Emerico (1989) "*In vitro* propagation of *Agapanthus umbellatus* L'Her. (= A. *africanus* Hoffm.) by culture and repeated subculture of different types of explants" ("Propagation *in vitro* d'*Agapanthus umbellatus* L'Her. [= A. *africanus* Hoffm.] par culture et repiquages répétés de divers types d'explants") in *Comptes Rendus des Séances de la Société de Biologie et de ses Filiales* 183, no. 3, p 193-202.

Other references:

Malho, R. and M.S.S. Pais (1992) "Kinetics and hydrodynamics of *Agapanthus umbellatus* pollen-tube growth: a structural and stereological study" in *Sexual Plant Reproduction* 5, no. 3, p 163-168.

Robbertse, P.J., J.J. Lock, E. Stoffberg and L.A. Coetzer (1990) "Effect of boron on directionality of pollen tube growth in *Petunia* and *Agapanthus*" in *South African Journal of Botany* 56, no. 4, p 487-492.

Botanical name: ***Aloe barbadiensis*** Mill.
(syn. *Aloe vera* L.)
Common name: Aloe

TECHNIQUES:

Micropropagation from vegetative meristems (Natali *et al*., 1990)

MS mineral salts and vitamin
sucrose 30 g l^{-1}
2,4-D 1.1 TM
KIN 2.3 TM
pH 5.7
agar 7 g l^{-1}

(after 60 days shoots will be propagated on the following medium)
MS mineral salts and vitamin
sucrose 30 g l^{-1}
2,4-D 0.11 TM
BA 2.2 TM
pH 5.7
agar 7 g l^{-1}

Bud growth and rooting of shoots (Meyer and van Staden, 1991)

MS salts and vitamin
sucrose 30 g l^{-1}
IBA 5 TM
pH 5.7
gelrite 2 g l^{-1}

Induction, growth and maintenance of callus tissues from young axillary shoot segment (Roy and Sarkar, 1991)

MS medium
PVP 1 g l^{-1}
2,4-D 1 mg l^{-1}
KIN 0.2 mg l^{-1}
pH 5.6 - 5.8
p-aminobenzoic acid 0.1 mg l^{-1}
agar

Shoot differentiation from callus (Roy and Sarkar, 1991)

MS medium
2,4-D 0.02 mg l^{-1}
KIN 1 mg l^{-1}
pH 5.6 - 5.8
agar

REFERENCES:

Meyer, H.J. and J. van Staden (1991) "Rapid *in vitro* propagation of *Aloe barbadiensis* Mill." in *Plant Cell, Tissue and Organ Culture* no. 26, p 167-171.

Natali L., I.C. Sanchez and A. Cavallini (1990) "*In vitro* culture of *Aloe barbadiensis* Mill.: micropropagation from vegetative meristems" in *Plant Cell, Tissue and Organ Culture*, no. 20, p 71-74.

Roy S.C. and A. Sarkar (1991) "*In vitro* regeneration and micropropagation of *Aloe vera* L." in *Sc. Horticolturae*, no. 47, p 107-113.

Botanical name: ***Alpinia purpurata*** (Vieill.) Schumann
Common name: Red ginger

TECHNIQUES:

Micropropagation of bulbils arising in the inflorescens (Dekkers *et al*., 1991)

MS medium
BA 4.4 TM
pH 5.7
agar 7 g l^{-1}

One year *in vitro* storage of bulbils arising in the inflorescens (Dekkers *et al*., 1991)

MS medium
BA 4.4 TM
pH 5.7
agar 7 g l^{-1}
liquid paraffin overlay (diluted autoclaved liquid paraffin, colourless light, viscosity < 30 centistokes, density 0.83-0.86 g ml^{-1}, GPR product 29436, BDH Ltd., Poole, UK)
12 h cool daylight fluorescent lighting at 10 TE m^{-2} s^{-1} at 28 ±1°C
12 h darkness at 25 ±1°C

REFERENCES:

Dekkers, A. J., A. N. Rao and C. J. Goh 1991 "*In vitro* storage of multiple shoot cultures of gingers at ambient temperatures of 24°- 29°C" in *Scientia Horticulturae* no. 47, p 157-167.

Botanical name: ***Anthurium x cultorum*** Birdsey
(syn. A. *andreanum* hort. non Linden)

Common name: Anthurium hybrids

TECHNIQUES:

Shoot growth from vegetative buds (Kunisaki, 1980)

(liquid medium)
Micro and macronutrients: MS
Vitamins: Kunisaki (1975)
sucrose 20 g l^{-1}
coconut milk 150 g l^{-1}
pH 5.8

Multiple shoots from 2-node stem sections (Kunisaki, 1980)

Micro and macronutrients: MS
Vitamins: Kunisaki (1975)
sucrose 20 g l^{-1}
BAP 0.2-1 mg l^{-1}
pH 5.8
agar 8 g l^{-1}

Rooted plantlets from shoots (Pierik *et al.*, 1974)

MS medium (macronutrients half strength)
sucrose 30 g l^{-1}
pH 5.8
agar 7 g l^{-1}

Somatic embryogenesis and plant regeneration (Kuehnle *et al.*, 1992)

- Embryogenic calli initiation from whole leaf blade explants

MS medium (half strength)
sucrose 20 g l^{-1}
glucose 10 g l^{-1}
2,4-D 1-4 mg l^{-1}
KIN 0.33-1.00 mg l^{-1}
pH 5.8
gelrite 1.8 g l^{-1}

- Somatic embryos from embryogenic calli

MS medium
sucrose 20 g l^{-1}
BA 0.2 mg l^{-1}
pH 5.8
gelrite 1.8 g l^{-1}
16 h photoperiod 54 TE m^{-2} s^{-1} at 25°C

REFERENCES:

Kuehnle, A., F.C. Chen and N. Sugii (1992) "Somatic embryogenesis and plant regeneration in *Anthurium andraeanum* hybrids" in *Plant Cell Reports* no. 11, p 438-442.

Kunisaki, J.T. (1980) "*In vitro* propagation of *Anthurium andreanum* Lind." in *HortScience* no. 15, p 508-509.

Pierik, R.L.M., H.H.M. Steegmans and J.A.J. Van der Meys (1974) "Plantlet formation in callus tissues of *Anthurium andreanum* Lind." in *Scientia Horticolturae* no. 2, p 193-198.

Other references:

Finnie, J.F. and J. Staden (1986) "*In vitro* culture of *Anthurium andreanum*" in *South African Journal of Botany* 52, no. 4, p 343-346.

Foja Singh (1991) "Micropropagation and plant conformity in *Anthurium andreanum*" in Proceedings of the International Seminar on New Frontiers in Horticulture, organized by Indo-American Hybrid Seeds, Bangalore, India, 25-28 Nov. 1990 (edited by J. Prakash and R.L.M. Pierik), Kluwer Academic Publishers (1991) in *Current plant science and biotechnology in agriculture* 12, p 201-204.

Kuehnle, A.R. and N. Sugii (1991) "Callus induction and plantlet regeneration in tissue cultures of Hawaiian anthuriums" in *HortScience* 26, no. 7, p 919-921.

Kuehnle, A.R. and G.L. Nan (1991) "Isolation and culture of protoplasts from two tropical monocots, *Anthurium* and *Dendrobium* orchid" (Abstract). Eighth international protoplast symposium in *Physiologia Plantarum* 82, no. 1, p. A7.

Kuehnle A., F.C. Chen and N. Sugii (1992) "Somatic embryogenesis and plant regeneration in *Anthurium andraeanum* hybrids" in *Plant Cell Reports* 11, no. 9, p 438-442.

Lightbourn G.J. and P.V.D. Prasad (1990) "*In vitro* techniques for rapid multiplication of four varieties of *Anthurium andraeanum* in Jamaica". XXXVI Annual meeting, Kingston, Jamaica, 27 April-3 May 1990 *in Jamaica Proceedings of the Interamerican Society for Tropical Horticulture* no. 34, p 3-5.

Soczek U. and M. Hempel (1989) "Effect of cytokinins on growth and development of *Anthurium x cultorum* Birdsey shoot explants *in vitro*". Third symposium on growth regulators in ornamental horticulture, Skierniewice, Poland, 10-15 Sept. 1988 in *Acta Horticulturae* no. 251, p 249-254.

Botanical name: ***Asclepias curassavica*** L.
Common name: Blood flower

TECHNIQUES:

Callus induction from twining stem segment (Prabhudesai and N'swami, 1974)

Macronutrients: MS
Micronutrients: Halperin (1966)
sucrose 20 g l^{-1}
2,4-D 2 mg l^{-1}
coconut milk 10 %
agar

REFERENCES:

Prabhundesai, V. and S. Narayanaswamy (1974) "Organogenesis in tissue cultures of certain asclepiads" in *Z. Pflanzenphysiology* no. 71, p 181-185.

Other references:

Dasgupta, M., T.K. Pramanik and S.K. Datta (1987) "Mass propagation and genetic variability of two cardenolide plants *in vitro*" in *Acta Horticulturae* no. 208, p 263-271.

Pramanik, T.K., S.K. Datta (1986) "Plant regeneration and ploidy variation in culture derived plants of *Asclepias curassavica* L." in *Plant Cell Reports* 5, no. 3, p 219-222.

Botanical name: ***Bauhinia variegata*** **L.**
Common name: Bauhinia

TECHNIQUES:

Shoot proliferation from nodal explants (Mathur and Makunthakumar, 1992)

MS medium
sucrose 30 g l^{-1}
myo-inositol 100 mg l^{-1}
BA 13.3 TM
pH 5.8
agar 7 g l^{-1}

Rooted plantlets from 3-4 nodes shoots (Mathur and Makunthakumar, 1992)

MS medium
sucrose 30 g l^{-1}
myo-inositol 100 mg l^{-1}
IBA 4.9 TM
pH 5.8
agar 7 g l^{-1}

REFERENCES:

Mathur, J. and S. Makunthakumar (1992) "Micropropagation of *Bauhinia variegata* and *Parkinsonia aculeata* from nodal explants of mature trees" in *Plant Cell, Tissue and Organ Culture* no. 28, p 119-121.

Botanical name: ***Bougainvillea glabra*** 'Magnifica'
Common name: Bougainvillea

TECHNIQUES:

Culture initiation from shoot tips (Chaturvedi *et al.*, 1978)

Macronutrients, vitamins, amino acids and amides: Chaturvedi *et al.* (1978)
Micronutrients: MS
sucrose 30 g l^{-1}
IAA 1 mg l^{-1}
BAP 0.2 mg l^{-1}
pH 5.8
agar 7 g l^{-1}

Shoot multiplication (Sharma *et al.*, 1981)

Macronutrients, vitamins, amino acids and amides: Chaturvedi *et al.* (1978)
Micronutrients: MS
sucrose 30 g l^{-1}
IAA 1.5 mg l^{-1}
BAP 0.5 mg l^{-1}
pH 5.8
agar 7 g l^{-1}

Rooted plantlets from shoots (Sharma *et al.*, 1981)

Macronutrients, amino acids and amides: Chaturvedi *et al.* (1978)
Micronutrients: MS
Vitamins: Sharma A.K. *et al.* (1981)
sucrose 30 g l^{-1}
IBA 0.1 mg l^{-1}
2,4,5-T 0.1 mg l^{-1}
pH 4.5
agar 7 g l^{-1}

REFERENCES:

Chaturvedi, H.C., A.K. Sharma and R.N. Prasad (1978) "Shoot apex culture of *Bouganvillea glabra* 'Magnifica'" in *HortScience* no. 13, p 36.
Sharma, A.K., R.N. Prasad and H.C. Chaturvedi (1981) "Clonal propagation of *Bouganvillea glabra* 'Magnifica' through shoot apex culture" in *Plant Cell, Tissue and Organ Culture* no. 1, p 33-38.

Botanical name: ***Caesalpinia pulcherrima*** (L.) Sw.
Common name: Barbados pride, Dwarf Poinciana

Techniques:

Micropropagation through nodal buds (Rahman *et al*., 1993)

- Shoots proliferation from nodal buds

MS medium
BA 4.5 TM (or KIN 4.5 TM)
NAA 5.5 TM
pH 5.8
Difco Bacto-agar 6 g l^{-1}
grown at: 25 ± 2°C; humidity 55-60%; 16h photoperiod (50-70 Tmol m^{-2} s^{-1} provided by warm white fluorescent tubes)

- Adventitious root induction

MS medium (half strength)
IAA 5.5 TM
pH 5.8
Difco Bacto-agar 6 g l^{-1}

References:

Rahman, S.M., M: Hossain, B.K. Biswas, O.I. Joarder and R. Islam (1993) "Micropropagation of *Caesalpinia pulcherrima* through nodal bud culture of mature tree" in *Plant Cell, Tissue and Organ Culture* 32, no. 3, p 363-365.

Botanical name: ***Calotropis gigantea*** (Linn.) R. Br.
Common name: Calotropis

TECHNIQUES:

Callus induction from immature embryos, shoot bud formation, growth and rooted plants (Roy and De, 1990)

- Callus induction from immature embryos (1.0-1.5 mm long embryos)

Basal medium (MS salts modified as follows:
NH_4NO_3 2 000 mg l^{-1}
KNO_3 2 400 mg l^{-1}
$CaCl_2$ 600 mg l^{-1})
sucrose 30 g l^{-1}
thiamine-HCl 4 mg l^{-1}
myo-inositol 300 mg l^{-1}
2,4-D 1 mg l^{-1}
pH 5.7
agar 8 g l^{-1}

- Shoot bud formation and growth from callus

Basal medium (see callus induction)
sucrose 30 g l^{-1}
thiamine-HCl 4 mg l^{-1}
myo-inositol 300 mg l^{-1}
NAA 0.1 mg l^{-1}
BAP 2.0 mg l^{-1}
pH 5.7
agar 8 g l^{-1}

- Rooted plantlets from shoots

Basal medium half strength (see callus induction)
sucrose 30 g l^{-1}
thiamine-HCl 4 mg l^{-1}
myo-inositol 300 mg l^{-1}
IBA 0.1 mg l^{-1}
pH 5.7
agar 8 g l^{-1}

REFERENCES:

Roy, A.T. and D.N. De (1990) "Tissue culture and plant regeneration from immature embryo explant of *Calotropsis gigantea* (Linn.) R. Br." In *Plant Cell, Tissue and Organ Culture* no. 20, p 229-233.

Botanical name: ***Cassia didymobotrya*** Fresen
Common name: Candle bush

TECHNIQUES:

Cell suspension cultures from seedling-derived callus (Botta *et al.*, 1989)

- Seed germination

MS basal salt medium
sucrose 30 g l^{-1}
pH 5.5
agar 9 g l^{-1}

- Callus induction from explants of hypocotyl and stem (5-7 day-old seedlings); suspension culture initiation and maintenance

MS basal salt medium
sucrose 30 g l^{-1}
2,4-D 1 mg l^{-1}
KIN 0.1 mg l^{-1}
pH 5.5
agar 9 g l^{-1} (only in callus induction)

(cell suspension was subcultured every 3 weeks)

REFERENCES:

Botta, B., G. Dall'Olio, F. Ferrari, B. Monacelli, G. Pasqua, R. Scurria and G. Delle Monache (1989) "Cell suspension cultures of *Cassia didymobotria*: optimization of growth and secondary metabolite production by application of the orthogonal design method" in *J. Plant Physiol*. no. 135, p 290-294.

Other references:

Bajaj, Y.P.S. (1993) "Biotechnology in agriculture and forestry 21" in *Medicinal and aromatic plants IV A-137*, Berlin, Germany, Springer-Verlag, p xxi + 443 pp.

Monache, G. delle, M.C. de Rosa, R. Scurria, B. Monacelli, G. Pasqua, G. Dall'Olio and B. Botta (1991) "Metabolites from *in vitro* cultures of *Cassia didymobotrya*" in *Phytochemistry* 30, no. 6, p 1849-1854.

Shah, R.R., K.V. Subbaiah and A.R. Mehta (1978) "Carbohydrate influence on polyphenol accumulation in *Cassia* and *Datura* tissues cultured *in vitro*" in *Biol. Pl.* No. 1, p 5-13.

Botanical name: ***Catharantus roseus*** (L.) G. Don
Common name: Madagascar Periwinkle

TECHNIQUES:

Callus growth from stem or pod (Ramawat *et al.*, 1978)

MS medium
sucrose 30 g l^{-1}
KIN 0.25-1 mg l^{-1}
NAA 0.25-5 mg l^{-1}
agar

Well-developed shoots from callus (Ramawat *et al.*, 1978)

MS medium
sucrose 30 g l^{-1}
KIN 2.5 mg l^{-1}
± NAA 0.05
pH 5.8
agar

REFERENCES:

Ramawat, K.G., R. Raj Bhansali and H.C. Harya (1978) "Shoot formation in *Catharanthus roseus* L. Don callus cultures" in *Current Science* no. 47, p 93-94.

Other references:

Berglund, T., A.B. Ohlsson and J. Rydström J. (1993) "Nicotinamide increases glutathione and anthocyanin in tissue culture of *Catharanthus roseus*" in *Journal of Plant Physiology* 141, Vol. 5, p 596-600.

Constabel, F., H. Koblitz, J.W. Kirkpatrik and S. Rambold (1980) "Fusion of cell sap vacuoles subsequent to protoplast fusion" in *Can. J. Bot.* no. 58, p 1032-1034.

Constabel, F., S. Rambold, K.B. Chatson, W.G.M. Kurz and J.P. Kutney (1982) "Alkaloid production in *Catharanthus roseus* (L.) G. Don. VI. Variation in alkaloid spectra of cell lines derived from one single leaf" in *Plant Cell Report* no. 1, p 3-5.

Hegarty, P.K., N.J. Smart, A.H. Scragg and M.W. Fowler (1986) "The aeration of *Catharanthus roseus* L.G.D. on suspension cultures in airlift bioreactor: the inhibitory effect at high aeration rates on culture growth" in *J. Exp. Bot.* no. 37, p 1911-1920.

Morris, P. and M.W. Fowler (1981) "A new method for the production of fine plant cell suspension cultures" in *Plant Cell, Tissue and Organ Culture* no. 1, p 15-24.

Renaudin, J.P. (1981) "Taberanthine by cell suspension cultures of *Catharanthus roseus* L.G.Don and *Acer pseudoplatanus* L." in *Plant Science Letter* no. 22, p 59-70.
Stafford, A., L. Smith and M.W. Foler (1985) "Regulation of product synthesis in cell culture of *Catharanthus roseus* (L.) G. Don. Growth related indole alkaloid accumulation in batch cultures" in *Plant Cell, Tissue and Organ Culture* no. 4, p 83-94.

Botanical name: ***Codiaeum variegatum*** L.
Common name Croton

TECHNIQUES:

Embryogenetic callus from isolated embryos (Chikkannaiah *et al*,. 1976)

Macro, micronutrients and vitamins: Ranga Swamy (1961)
Aminoacids and amides: Johri and Bajaj (1962)
sucrose 20 g l^{-1}
2,4-D 1 mg l^{-1}
coconutmilk 10 %
pH 5.8
agar 8 g l^{-1}

REFERENCES:

Chikkannaiah, P.S., K. Nataraja and M.C. Gayatri (1976) "Response of seeds and isolated embryos of *Codiaeum variegatum in vitro*" in *Current Science* no. 45, p 196-197.

Other references:

Chikkannaiah, P.S. and M.C. Gayatri (1974) "Organogenesis in endosperm tissue cultures of *Codiaeum variegatum* Blume" in *Current Science* no. 43, p 23-24.

Botanical name: ***Cordyline fruticosa*** (L.) A. Chev. (syn. *C. terminalis* L. Kunth)
Common name: Good-luck plant, Tree-of-Kings

TECHNIQUES:

Shoots production from axillary buds (Welander, 1988)

MS medium
sucrose 30 g l^{-1}
NAA 0.7 mg l^{-1}
BA 0.5 mg l^{-1}
agar 6 g l^{-1}

Shoots micropropagation (Paek *et al*,. 1985)

MS medium
IAA 1.0 mg l^{-1}
KIN 3.0 mg l^{-1}
adenine sulphate 100 mg l^{-1}
$Na_2H_2PO_4 \cdot H_2O$ 150 mg l^{-1}
agar
light intensity 500-1500 lux

REFERENCES:

Paek, K.Y., M.O. Oh and J.K. Choi (1985) "Mass propagation of *Cordyline* and *Scindapsus in vitro*" in *Journal of the Korean Society for Horticultural Science* 26, no. 1, p 83-92. (In Korean; summary in English.)

Welander, T. (1988) "Micropropagation of *Cordyline terminalis* cv. Atoom - a European cooperation project" in *Sveriges Lantbruksuniversitet* no. 54, p 13.

Other references:

Evaldsson, I.E. and N.T. Welander (1985) "The effects of medium composition on *in vitro* propagation and in vivo growth of *Cordyline terminalis* cv. Atoom" in *Journal of Horticultural Science*, 60, no. 4, p 525-530.

Kunisaki, J.T. (1975) "*In vitro* propagation of *Cordyline terminalis* L. Kunth" in *HortScience* no. 10, p 601-602.

Mee, G.W.P. (1978) "Propagation of *Cordyline terminalis* from callus culture" in *HortScience* no. 13, p 660.

Maene, L.J. and P.C. Debergh (1987) "Optimalisation of the transfer of tissue cultured shoots to *in vivo* conditions" in *Acta Horticulturae* no. 212, Vol. I., p 335-348.

Miller, L.R. and T. Murashige (1976) "Tissue culture propagation of tropical foliage plants" in *In vitro* no. 12, p 797-813.

Botanical name: ***Costus speciosus*** (Koenig) Smith
Common name: Crape ginger

TECHNIQUES:

Shoots proliferation from rhizome shoot tips (Chaturvedi *et al.*, 1984)

Macronutrients, vitamins, amino acids and amides: Chaturvedi *et al.* (1984)
Micronutrients: SH
sucrose 20 g l^{-1}
IAA 1 mg l^{-1}
BAP 0.5 mg l^{-1}
pH 5.2
agar

Rooted plantlets from shoots (Chaturvedi *et al.*, 1984)

Macronutrients, vitamins, amino acids and amides: Chaturvedi *et al.* (1984)
Micronutrients: SH
sucrose 20 g l^{-1}
IAA 1 mg l^{-1}
pH 5.2
agar

Multiple shoots from mature embryos (Pal and Roy, 1991b)

SH medium
KIN 0.1 mg l^{-1}
IBA 0.1 mg l^{-1}
agar

Rhizome development from stem cuttings (Pal and Roy, 1991a)

SH medium
casamino acids (CA) 250 mg l^{-1}
agar

Rhizome callus, caulogenesis, shoot development and shoot rooting from rhizome tissue explants (Jain and Chaturvedi, 1985)

- Rhizome callus and caulogenesis from rhizome tissue explants

SH medium
adenine sulphate 10 mg l^{-1}
BA 0.25 mg l^{-1}
IAA 0.5 mg l^{-1}
malt extract 100 mg l^{-1}
agar

- Shoots development

SH medium
IAA 2 mg l^{-1}
adenine sulphate 15 mg l^{-1}
BA 0.25 mg l^{-1}
malt extract 200 mg l^{-1}
agar

- Rooted plantlets from shoots

SH medium
IAA 3 mg l^{-1}
agar

REFERENCES:

Chaturvedi, H.C., P. Misra and M. Jain (1984) "Proliferation of shoot tips and clonal multiplication of *Costus speciosus* in long term culture" in *Plant Science Letter* no. 35, p 67-71.

Jain, M. and H.C. Chaturvedi (1985) "Caulogenesis in rhizome callus of *Costus speciosus*" in *Planta Medica* no. 5, p 462-463.

Pal, A. and A. Roy (1991a) "Propagation of *Costus speciosus* (Koen.) Sm. through *in vitro* rhizome production" in *Plant Cell Reports* 10, no. 10, p 525-528.

Pal, A. and A. Roy (1991b) "Embryo culture of *Costus speciosus* (Koen.) Sm. to regenerate variable diosgenin yielding clones" in *Plant Cell Reports* 10, no. 11, p 565-568.

Other references:

Li, Z.S., J. Attias and B. Marin (1992) "Estimation of the nucleotide pools of plant cells by high performance liquid chromatography: effect of column temperature and elution pH" in *Comptes Rendus de l'Academie des Sciences*, Series 3, 315, no. 3, p 127-132.

Botanical name: ***Euphorbia fulgens*** Karw. ex Klotsch
Common name: Scarlet plume

TECHNIQUES:

Shoot proliferation from nodal section of actively growing apical shoot (Zhang and Stoltz, 1989b)

MS medium
sucrose 130-160 mM
Z 5.0 TM
pH 5.3
agar

REFERENCES:

Zhang, B. and L.P. Stoltz (1989b) "Shoot proliferation of *Euphorbia fulgens in vitro* affected by medium components" in *HortScience* 24, no. 3, p 503-504.

Other references:

Zhang, B., L.P. Stoltz and J.C. Snyder (1987) "In vitro propagation of *Euphorbia fulgens*" in *HortScience* 22, no. 3, p 468-486.

Zhang, B. and L.P. Stoltz (1989a) "Acclimatization systems for *Euphorbia fulgens* microcuttings" in *HortScience* 24, no. 6, p 1025-1026.

Botanical name: ***Euphorbia pulcherrima*** Willd.
Common name: Poinsettia, Christmas star

TECHNIQUES:

Plants via direct adventitious shoots from seedling hypocotyl (Nataraja *et al*., 1973)

Ranga Swamy medium 1961
sucrose 20 g l^{-1}
2,4-D 1 mg l^{-1}
KIN 1 mg l^{-1}
coconut milk 10%
agar

Embryogenic callus from seed embryo (Nataraja *et al*., 1973)

(The same medium as above)

REFERENCES:

Nataraja, K., M.S. Chennaveeraiah and P. Girigowda (1973) "*In vitro* production of shoot buds in *Euphorbia pulcherrima*" in *Curr. Sci.* no. 42, p 577-578.

Other references:

Geier, T., A. Beck and W. Preil (1992) "High uniformity of plants regenerated from cytogenetically variable embryogenic suspension cultures of poinsettia (*Euphorbia pulcherrima* Willd. ex Klotzsch)" in *Plant Cell Reports* 11, no. 3, p 150-154.

Preil, W., P. Florek, U. Wix and A. Beck (1988) "Towards mass propagation by use of bioreactors", International symposium on propagation of ornamental plants, Geisenheim, German Federal Republic, 23-29 Aug. 1987, in *Acta Horticulturae* 226, Vol. I, p 99-106.

Botanical name: ***Gloriosa superba*** **L.**
Common name: Glory lily

TECHNIQUES:

Callus formation from embryos, tubers or seedlings (Finnie and Staden, 1989)

MS medium
sucrose 30 g l^{-1}
2,4-D 1 mg l^{-1}
KIN 1 mg l^{-1}
agar 8 g l^{-1}

Multiple plantlet production from mature tubers (Finnie and Staden, 1989)

MS medium
sucrose 30 g l^{-1}
NAA 0.25 mg l^{-1}
BA or KIN 2.5 mg l^{-1}
agar 8 g l^{-1}

REFERENCES:

Finnie, J.F. and J. van Staden (1989) "*In vitro* propagation of *Sandersonia* and *Gloriosa*" in *Plant Cell, Tissue and Organ Culture* no. 19, p 151-158.

Other references:

Somani, V.J., C.K. John and R.J. Thengane (1989) "*In vitro* propagation and corm formation in *Gloriosa superba* L." in *Indian Journal of Experimental Biology*, 27, no. 6, p 578-579.

Botanical name: ***Guzmania lingulata*** (L.) Mez
Common name: Guzmania

TECHNIQUES:

Optimal seedling growth from seeds (Pierik *et al*., 1984)

> Macronutrients: MS half strength
> Micronutrients: Pierik (1975)
> Vitamins: Mekers (1977)
> Amino acids and amides: Gresshoff and Doy (1972)
> sucrose 25 g l^{-1}
> NAA 0.5 mg l^{-1}
> pH 6.0
> agar 9 g l^{-1}

Multiplication of plantlets (Mekers, 1977)

> MS medium (also diluted 1:2 or 1:3 of the normal salt concentration)
> sucrose 20 g l^{-1}
> meso-inositol 100 mg l^{-1}
> nicotinic acid 5 mg l^{-1}
> thiamin-HCl 5 mg l^{-1}
> pyridoxine-HCl 0.5 mg l^{-1}
> glycine 4.0 mg l^{-1}
> NAA 1 mg l^{-1}
> BAP 1 mg l^{-1}
> adenine 40 mg l^{-1}
> pH 5.5
> agar

REFERENCES:

Mekers, O. (1977) "In vitro propagation of some Thillansoideae (Bromeliaceae)" *Acta Hort.* No. 78, p 311-320.

Pierik, R.L.M., H.H.M. Steegmans and J. Hendriks (1984) "The influence of naphtaleneacetic acid on the growth of in vitro cultivated seedlings of Bromeliaceae" in *Scientia Hort.* no. 24, p 193-199.

Botanical name: ***Heliconia psittacorum*** L.
Common name: Parrot's plantain

TECHNIQUES:

Propagation by bud culture (Nathan *et al.*, 1992)

MS inorganic salt medium
thiamine-HCl 0.5 mg l^{-1}
myo-inositol 100 mg l^{-1}
sodium hydrogen phosphate 170 mg l^{-1}
adenine sulphate 80 mg l^{-1}
sucrose 30 g l^{-1}
BA 40 TM
coconut water 150 ml l^{-1}
pH 5.7
gelrite 2 g l^{-1}

(after 3-4 months shoot will be tansferred on the following medium)
MS inorganic salt medium
thiamine-HCl 0.5 mg l^{-1}
myo-inositol 100 mg l^{-1}
sodium hydrogen phosphate 170 mg l^{-1}
adenine sulphate 80 mg l^{-1}
sucrose 30 g l^{-1}
BA TM
pH 5.7
Gelrite 2 g l^{-1}

High frequency plant regeneration from shoot tips derived callus (Nathan *et al.*, 1993)

(in the dark on semisolid medium)
MS medium
activated charcoal 0.5 g l^{-1}
casein hydrolysate 1.0 g l^{-1}
2,4-D 80 TM

Reducing the concentration of 2,4-D in the medium to 40 TM and subculturing at 6-week intervals enabled long-term maintenance of this regenerative callus.

REFERENCES:

Nathan, M.J., P.P. Kumar and G.J. Goh (1993) "High frequency plant regeneration in *Heliconia psittacorum* L." in *Plant Science (Limerick)*, 90, no. 1, p 63-71.

Nathan, M.J., C.J. Goh and P.P. Kumar (1992) "*In vitro* propagation of *Heliconia psittacorum* by bud culture" in *HortScience* 27, no. 5, p 450-452.

Botanical name: ***Jatropha panduraefolia*** Andr. (syn. J. integerrima Jacq.)
Common name: Peregrina

TECHNIQUES:

Adventitious shoot and root formation from subcultured embryo-derived callus (Srivastava and Johri, 1974)

- Callus from endosperm and embryo

Macro, micronutrients and vitamins: Ranga Swami (1961)
Amino acids and amides: Satsangi and Mohan Ram (1965)
sucrose 20 g l^{-1}
2,4-D 2 mg l^{-1}
KIN 5 mg l^{-1}
agar

- Adventitious shoot and root from subcultured callus

Macro, micronutrients and vitamins: Ranga Swami (1961)
Amino acids and amides: Johri and Bajaj (1962)
sucrose 20 mg l^{-1}
NAA 0.5 mg l^{-1}
KIN 0.5 mg l^{-1}
agar

Direct shoot regeneration, rooting and propagation, from different explants (Sujatha and Dhingra, 1993)

- Shoot regeneration

MS medium
sucrose 30 g l^{-1}
BA 2.2 or 4.4 TM
IBA 4.9 TM (IBA 2.5 TM promotes further development of shoots)
pH 5.8
agar 7 g l^{-1}

- Rooted plantlets from shoots

MS medium
sucrose 30 g l^{-1}
pH 5.8
agar 7 g l^{-1}

REFERENCES:

Srivastava, P.S. and J.M. Johri (1974) "Morphogenesis in mature endosperm cultures of *Jatropa panduraefolia*" in *Beitr. Biol. Pflanz.*, no. 50, p 255-268

Sujatha, M. and Mukta Dhingra (1993) "Rapid plant regeneration from various explants of *Jatropa integerrima*" in *Plant Cell, Tissue and Organ Culture* no. 35, p 293-296.

Other references:

Johri, B.M. and S.S. Bhojwani (1965) "Growth responses of mature endosperm in cultures" in *Nature* no. 208, p 1345-1347.

Jhori, B.M. and P.S. Srivastava (1973) "Morphogenesis in endosperm cultures" in *Z. Pflanzenphysiol.* no. 70, p 285-304.

Srivastava, P.S. (1971) "*In vitro* induction of triploid roots and shoots from mature endosperm of *Jatropa panduraefolia*" in *Z. Pflanzenphysiol.* no. 66, p 93-96.

Botanical name: ***Liatris spicata*** L.
Common name: Blazing star, Gay feather

TECHNIQUES:

Shoot proliferation from stem (Stimart and Harbage, 1989)

MS medium
BA 2.7 TM
Difco Bacto-agar 6 g l^{-1}

Rooted plantlets from shoots (Stimart and Harbage, 1989)

MS medium
IBA 5.0 TM
Difco Bacto-agar 6 g l^{-1}

REFERENCES:

Stimart, D.P. and J.F. Harbage (1989) "Shoot proliferation and rooting *in vitro* of *Liatris spicata*" in *HortScience*, 24, 5, p 835-836.

Botanical name: ***Momordica charantia*** **L.**
Common name: Balsam pear

TECHNIQUES:

Morphogenesis (Halder and Gadgil, 1982)

- Seeds germination

White medium 1954
sucrose 20 g l^{-1}
agar

- Callus growth from hypocotyl and subsequent subcultures

MS medium
sucrose 20 g l^{-1}
NAA 2 mg l^{-1} (later 1 mg l^{-1})
coconut milk 15%
pH 5.8
agar

- Shoot buds (and callus production) from callus

MS medium
sucrose 20 g l^{-1}
NAA 0.1-1 mg l^{-1}
adenine (anhydrous) 33.8 mg l^{-1}
pH 5.8
agar

REFERENCES:

Halder, T. and V.N. Gadgil (1982) "Morphogenesis in some plant species of the family *Cucurbitaceae*" in Rao A.N. (ed.) 1982, *Tissue Culture of Economically Important Plants*, Proc. of Int. Symp. Singapore 1981, COSTED and ANBS, p 98-103.

Botanical name: ***Mussaenda erythrophylla*** Schum. & Thonn.
Common name: Red flag bush

TECHNIQUES:

Callus and regeneration from segments (0.3-0.5 mm) of midrib and petiole (Panda *et al.*, 1989)

- Callus production from segments (0.3-0.5 mm) of midrib and petiole

MS medium
sucrose 30 g l^{-1}
BA 0.5 mg l^{-1}
ascorbic acid 10 mg l^{-1}
agar

- Shoot regeneration from callus

MS medium
sucrose 30 g l^{-1}
BA 3 mg l^{-1}
IAA 2 mg l^{-1}
ascorbic acid 10 g l^{-1}.
agar

- Shoots propagation

MS medium
sucrose 30 g l^{-1}
adenine sulphate 40 mg l^{-1}
agar

- Rooting shoots

MS medium
sucrose 30 g l^{-1}
NAA 0.5 mg l^{-1}
agar

Shoot proliferation (Cramer and Bridgen, 1993)

MS salts media
sucrose 30 g l^{-1}
myo-inositol 100 mg l^{-1}
thiamine-HCl 0.4 mg l^{-1}

BAP 10 Tm
adenine sulphate 217 TM
pH 5.8
agar 7 g l^{-1}

REFERENCES:

Cramer, C.S. and M.P. Bridgen (1993) "*In vitro* shoot proliferation of *Mussaenda* 'Dona Luz'" in *HortScience* no. 28, p 447.

Panda, N., B.K Debata and P. Das (1989) "*In vitro* regeneration of *Mussaenda erythrophylla* cvs 'Queen Sirikit' and 'Rosea' from callus cultures" in *Orissa Journal of Horticulture* 17, nos 1-2, p 18-22.

Other references:

Das, P., G.R. Rout and A.B. Das (1993) "Somatic embryogenesis in callus culture of *Mussaenda erythrophylla* cvs. 'Queen Sirikit' and 'Rosea' in *Plant Cell, Tissue and Organ Culture* no. 35, p 199-201.

Botanical name:	***Neoregelia carolinae*** (Mez) L.B. Smith var. tricolor L.B. Smith
Common name:	Neoregelia

TECHNIQUES:

Shoots proliferation from meristems (Tombolato *et al.*, 1991)

(on a filter paper bridge)
MS medium
sucrose 30 g l^{-1}

(after 30-40 days explants will be subcultured as follows)
MS medium
sucrose 30 g l^{-1}
NAA 0.2 mg l^{-1}
BA 0.2 mg l^{-1}
agar 7 g l^{-1}

(after 2 months shoots will be transferred as follows)
MS medium
sucrose 30 g l^{-1}
NAA 2 mg l^{-1}
BA 2 mg l^{-1}
agar 7 g l^{-1}

Rooted plantlets from shoots (Tombolato *et al.*, 1991)

MS medium
sucrose 30 g l^{-1}

REFERENCES:

Tombolato, A.F.C., S.S.G. Takebayashi, A.M.M. Costa and E. Quirino (1991) "*In vitro* culture of bromeliads" in *Brazil Agronomico* 43, nos 2-3, p 77-78.

Botanical name: ***Passiflora caerulea*** **L.**
Common name: Blue passion flower

TECHNIQUES:

Rapid growth of juvenile shoots (Drew, 1991)

MS medium
sucrose 20 g l^{-1}
KIN 10 TM
IAA 5 TM
pH 5.8
Difco Bacto-agar 8 g l^{-1}

Rooted plantlets from shoots (Drew, 1991)

MS medium
sucrose 20 g l^{-1}
IAA 5 TM
pH 5.8
Difco Bacto-agar 8 g l^{-1}

Callus initiation from leaf discs and shoot initials (Scorza and Janik, 1979)

Macro and micronutrients: MS
Vitamins: Hall and Collin (1975)
Amino acids and amides: Gresshoff and Doy (1972)
sucrose 30 g l^{-1}
NAA 1 mg l^{-1}
BAP 1 mg l^{-1} (only in callus initiation)
pH 5.8
agar

REFERENCES:

Drew, R.A. (1991) "*In vitro* culture of adult and juvenile bud explants of *Passiflora* species" in *Plant Cell, Tissue and Organ Culture*, 26, no. 1, p 23-27.
Scorza, R. and J. Janik (1979) "Tissue culture in *Passiflora*" in *24th Ann. Cong. Am. Soc. Hort. Sci. Trop. Reg. 1976*, p 179-183.

Other references:

Montaldi, E.R. (1972) "Kinetin induction of bud differentiation on roots of entire plants" in *Z. Pflanzenphysiol*. no. 67, p 43-44.

Botanical name: ***Plumbago indica*** **L.**
Common name: Plumbago

TECHNIQUES:

Vegetative shoots from stem section (Nitsch and Nitsch, 1967)

Macronutrients: Knop 1865 half strength
Micronutrients and vitamins: Nitsch and Nitsch (1965)
Amino acids and amides: MS
sucrose 10 g l^{-1}
KIN 1 mg l^{-1}
adenine (anhydrous) 40.5 mg l^{-1}
agarose 10 g l^{-1}

Adventitious flower buds from stem segments (Nitsch, 1968)

Macronutrients, amino acids and amides: MS
Micronutrients: Bourgin and Nitsch (1967)
Vitamins: Nitsch and Nitsch (1965)
sucrose 30 g l^{-1}
Z 0.2 mg l^{-1}
adenine sulphate (dihydrate) 40 mg l^{-1}
agar 8 g l^{-1}

REFERENCES:

Nitsch, C. and J.P. Nitsch (1967a) "The induction of flowering *in vitro* in stem segments of *Plumbago indica* L. II. The production of vegetative buds" in *Planta* no. 72, p 355-370.

Nitsch, C. (1968) "Induction *in vitro* de la floraison chez une plante de jour courts: *Plumbago indica* L." in *Ann. Sci. Nat. Bot. Paris*, 12th Series, no. 9, p 1-91.

Other references:

Nitsch, C. and J.P. Nitsch (1967b) "The induction of flowering *in vitro* in stem segments of *Plumbago indica* L. II. The production of reproductive buds" in *Planta* no. 72, p 371-384.

Nitsch, J.P. (1965) "Deux espèces photopériodique de jour courts: *Plumbago indica* L. et *P. zeylanica* L." in *Bull. Soc. Bot. France* no. 112, p 517-522.

Nitsch, J.P. and C. Nitsch (1965) "Néoformation de fleurs in vitro chez une espèce de jour courts: *Plumbago indica* L." in *Ann. Phys. Vég*. no. 7, p 251-256.

Nitsch, J.P., C. Nitsch, L.M.E. Rossini and D. Bui Dng Ha (1967) "The role of adenine in bud differentiation" in *Phytomorph*. no. 17, p 446-453.

Botanical name: ***Strelitzia reginae*** Banks
Common name: Bird of paradise flower

TECHNIQUES:

Shoot proliferation and callus from stem node (Ziv and Halevy, 1983)

MS medium (macronutrients half strength)
sucrose 30 g l^{-1}
NAA 1 mg l^{-1}
IBA 2.5 mg l^{-1}
2,4-D 0.5 mg l^{-1}
KIN 5 mg l^{-1}
pH 5.8
activated charcoal 1%
agar

Shoot growth from shoot cluster (Ziv and Halevy, 1983)

(liquid medium)
MS medium (macronutrients half strength)
sucrose 30 g l^{-1}
IBA 5.0
BAP 1.0
dithiothreitol 0.04 %
pH 5.8

REFERENCES:

Ziv, M. and A.H. Halevy (1983) "Control of oxidative browning and *in vitro* propagation of *Strelitzia reginae*" in *HortScience* no. 18, p 434-436.

Botanical name: ***Thevetia peruviana*** (Pers.) Schum.
Common name: Yellow oleander

TECHNIQUES:

Somatic embryogenesis and high frequency plantlet regeneration in young leaf discs derived callus (Anjani Kumar, 1992)

- Callus production from 30-day-old leaf discs

MS medium
2,4-D 9.0 TM
KIN 4.6 TM

- Callus subcultures

MS medium
2,4-D 4.5 TM
KIN 0.46 TM

- Production of somatic embryos from callus after 30-45 days

MS medium
KIN 9.26 TM (or 2iP 5.95 TM)
2,4-D 0.45 TM

REFERENCES:

Anjani Kumar (1992) "Somatic embryogenesis and high frequency plantlet regeneration in callus cultures of *Thevetia peruviana*" in *Plant Cell, Tissue and Organ Culture* 31, no. 1, p 47-50.

Other references:

Anjani Kumar (1990) "Investigation on *in vitro* laticifer differentiation in *Thevetia peruviana* L." in *Phytomorphology*, 40, nos 1-2, p 113-117.

Barros, A.M., L. Cosson, M. Foulquier, S. Labidalle, J. Osuku-Opio, H. Galons, M. Miocque and A. Jacquin-Dubreuil (1992) "Biotransformation of ethyl 2-acetylamino-2-carbethoxy-4-(phenylsulphinyl-)-butanoate by cell suspensions of *Catharanthus roseus* and *Thevetia neriifolia* Dantas" in *Phytochemistry* 31, no. 6, p 2019-2020.

Chatterjee, M., G. Ghosh and P.C. Datta (1987) "Role of exogenous cholesterol on *in vitro* secondary metabolism in *Thevetia peruviana* (Pers.) Schum." in *Indian Journal of Experimental Biology* 25, no. 3, p 204-206.

Dasgupta, M., T.K. Pramanik, S.K. Datta (1987) "Mass propagation and genetic variability of two cardenolide plants *in vitro*" in *Acta Horticulturae* no. 208, p 263-271.

Kreis, W., U. May and E. Reinhard (1986) "UDP-glucose: digitoxin 16'-O-glucosyltransferase from suspension-cultured *Digitalis lanata* cells" in *Plant Cell Reports* 5, no. 6, p. 7442-7445.

APPENDIX 1 - ABBREVIATIONS

2iP	N^6-(2-isopentyl)adenine
2,4-D	2,4-dichlorophenoxyacetic acid
2,4,5-T	2,4,5-trichlorophenoxyacetic acid
BA or BAP	6-benzylaminopurine
IAA	3-indoleacetic acid
IBA	3-indolebutyric acid
KIN	Kinetin; 6-furfurylaminopurine
MS medium	Murashige and Skoog 1962 (see Appendix 2)
NAA	1-naphtylacetic acid
PVP	Polyvinylpyrrolidone
SH medium	Schenk and Hildebrandt 1972 (see Appendix 2)
Z	Zeatin; 4-hydroxy-3-methyl-trans-2-butenylaminopurine

APPENDIX 2 – MEDIA COMPOSITIONS

MACRONUTRIENTS :

Macronutrient	Chaturvedi *et al.* 1978/1984	Knop 1865	Murashige and Skoog 1962 (MS)	Ranga Swamy 1961	Schenk and Hildebrandt 1972 (SH)	White 1954
KNO_3	500/1 000	250	1 900	80	2 500	80
NH_4NO_3	1 500		1 650			
$Ca(NO_3)_2 \cdot 4H_2O$		1 000		260		287.8
$CaCl_2 \cdot 2H_2O$	200		440		200	
$MgSO_4 \cdot 7H_2O$	100/400	250	370	360	400	737.1
KCl				65		65
KH_2PO_4	170/0	250	170			
$NH_4H_2PO_4$	0/300				300	
$NaH_2PO_4 \cdot H_2O$				189.8		19
Na_2SO_4				200		200

Note: All quantities are in mg l^{-1}

MICRONUTRIENTS :

Micronutrient	Bourgin and Nitsch 1967	Gresshoff and Doy 1972	Halperin 1966	Murashige and Skoog 1962 (MS)	Nitsch 1968	Nitsch and Nitsch 1965
$MnSO_4.4H_2O$	25 000	13 200	22 300	22 300	25 000	25 000
$ZnSO_4.7H_2O$	10 000	3 000	8 600	8 600	10 000	10 000
H_3BO_4	10 000	3 000	6 200	6 200	10 000	10 000
KI		750	830	830		
$CuSO_4.5H_2O$	25	250	25	25	25	25
$NaMoO_4.2H_2O$	250	250	250	250	250	250
$CoCl_2.6H_2O$		250	25	25		25
Ferric citrate					10 000	
$FeSO_4.7H_2O$	27 850	27 850	13 925	27 850		27 850
$Na_2EDTA.2H_2O$	37 250	37 250	18 625	37 250		37 250
NaFeEDTA						

Note: All quantities are in Tg l^{-1}

MICRONUTRIENTS:

Micronutrient	Pierik 1975	Ranga Swamy 1961	Ringe and Nitsch 1968	Schenk and Hildebrandt 1972 (SH)	Stoltz 1979	White 1954
$MnSO_4.4H_2O$	22 300	3 000	25 000	13 200	7 000	6 648
$ZnSO_4.7H_2O$	8 600	500	10 000	1 000	3 000	2 672
H_3BO_4	6 200	500	10 000	5 000	1 500	1 500
KI	830		1 000	1 000	750	750
$CuSO_4.5H_2O$	25	25	25	200		
$NaMoO_4.2H_2O$	250	29.375	250	100		
$CoCl_2.6H_2O$	25	45.812	25	100		
Ferric citrate		10 000				
$FeSO_4.7H_2O$			27 580	15 000	25 000	
$Fe_2(SO_4)_3$						2500
NaFeEDTA	25 000					
$Na_2EDTA.2H_2O$			37 250	20 000		
EDTA					26 200	

Note: All quantities are in Tg l^{-1}

VITAMINS:

Vitamin	Chaturvedi et al. 1978/1984	Gresshoff and Doy 1972	Hall and Collin 1975	Halperin 1966	Kunisaki 1975	Mekers 1977
Inositol (mg l^{-1})	100/0	10	200		100	100
Thiamine.HCl	100/5 000	1 000	200	3 000	400	5 000
Nicotinic ac.	500/5 000	100	1 000	5 000	500	5 000
Pyridoxine.HCl	100/500	100	1 000		500	500
Biotin	100/0					
Ascorbic ac.	5 000/0					

Vitamin	Murashige and Skoog 1962 (MS)	Nitsch and Nitsch 1965	Ranga Swamy 1961	Schenk and Hildebrandt 1972 (SH)	Sharma A.K. et al. 1981	White 1954
Inositol (mg l^{-1})	100	100		1 000		
Thiamine.HCl	100	500	250	5 000	100	100
Nicotinic ac.	500	5 000	1 250	5 000	500	500
Pyridoxine.HCl	500	500	25	500	100	100
Ca-pantothenate			25			
Biotin		50			100	
Folic ac.		500				
Ascorbic ac.					5 000	

Note: Quantities are in Tg l^{-1} except for inositol

AMINO ACIDS AND AMIDE:

Amino Acids and Amide	Chaturvedi et al. 1978/1984	Gresshoff and Doy 1972	Hall and Collin 1975	Johri and Bajaj 1962	Murashige and Skoog 1962 (MS)
Glycine	2.0/5.0	4.0	4.0	7.5	2.0
Arginine	10.0/5.0				
Glutamine	0.0/10.0				
Protein Hydrolysates			2 000.0	1 000.0	1 000.0

Aminoacids and amide	Nitsch and Nitsch 1965	Ranga Swamy 1961	Satsangi and Mohan Ram 1965	White 1954
Glycine	2.0	7.5	7.5	3.0
Glutamine	200.0			
Yeast/Malt Extract			2 500.0	

Note: All quantities are in mg l^{-1}

APPENDIX 3 – RECOMMENDED FURTHER READING

Bhojwani, S.S. and M.K. Razdan (1983) *Plant tissue culture: theory and practice*, Elsevier, Amsterdam.

Conger, B.V. (1981) *Cloning agricultural plants via in vitro techniques*, CRC Press, 2 000 N.W. 24th Street, Boca Raton, Florida.

Dirr, M.A. and C.W. Heuser Jr. (1987) *The reference manual of woody plant propagation: from seed to tissue culture. A practical working guide to the propagation of over 1100 species, varieties and cultivars*, Varsity Press, Athens, GA (USA).

Drew, R., M. Smith, J. Moisander and J. James (1991) *Plant tissue culture: general principles and commercial applications*, Queensland Department of Primary Industries, Australia GPO Box 46, Brisbane 4001.

Evans *et al* (1983 and following) *Handbook of plant cell culture* (six volumes), MacMillan Publisher, New York.

Green, C.E., D.A. Soners, W.P. Hackett and D.D. Biesboer (1986) *Plant tissue and cell culture*, Alan Liss Inc., New York.

Hartmann, H.T., D.E. Kester, F.T. Davies (1990) *Plant propagation: principles and practices*, Prentice Hall, Englewood Cliffs, NJ (USA).

Kyte, L. (1987) *Plants from test tubes*, Timber Press.

Margarà, J. (1989) *Bases de la multiplication vegetative*, INRA, 149 rue de Grenelle, 75341 Paris Cedex, France.

Pierik, R.L.M. (1987) *In vitro culture of higher plants*, Martinus Nijhoff Publishers, Kluwer Group, Dordrecht.

Reinert, J. and Y.P.S. Bajaj (1977) *Plant cell, tissue and organ culture*, Springer Verlag, Berlin, Heidelberg, New York.

Zimmerman, R.H. and P. Debergh. (1981) *Micropropagation*, Kluwer Publisher, Dordrecht.

Zyrd, J.P. (1988) *Cultures des cellules, tissus, et organes végétaux*, Presses polytechnique romandes, CH-1015 Lousanne.

BIBLIOGRAPHY

Anjani Kumar (1990) "Investigation on *in vitro* laticifer differentiation in *Thevetia peruviana* L." in *Phytomorphology* 40, nos 1-2, p 113-117.

Anjani Kumar (1992) "Somatic embryogenesis and high frequency plantlet regeneration in callus cultures of *Thevetia peruviana*" in *Plant Cell, Tissue and Organ Culture* 31, no. 1, p 47-50.

Apollonio, G., F. Scaramuzzi and S. D'Emerico (1989) "*In vitro* propagation of *Agapanthus umbellatus* L'Her. (= *A. africanus* Hoffm.) by culture and repeated subculture of different types of explants" (Propagation *in vitro d'Agapanthus umbellatus* L'Her. [= *A. africanus* Hoffm.] par culture et repiquages repetes de divers types d'explants) in *Comptes Rendus des Seances de la Societe de Biologie et de ses Filiales* 183, no. 3, p 193-202.

Bajaj, Y.P.S. (1993) "Biotechnology in agriculture and forestry 21" in *Medicinal and aromatic plants* IV A-137, Berlin, Germany, Springer-Verlag, p xxi + 443 pp.

Barros, A.M., L. Cosson, M. Foulquier, S. Labidalle, J. Osuku-Opio, H. Galons, M. Miocque and A. Jacquin-Dubreuil (1992) "Biotransformation of ethyl 2-acetylamino-2-carbethoxy-4-(phenylsulphinyl-)-butanoate by cell suspensions of *Catharanthus roseus* and *Thevetia neriifolia* Dantas" in *Phytochemistry* 31, no. 6, p 2019-2020.

Berglund, T., A.B. Ohlsson and J. Rydström (1993) "Nicotinamide increases glutathione and anthocyanin in tissue culture of *Catharanthus roseus*" in *Journal of Plant Physiology* 141, no. 5, p 596-600.

Botta, B., G. Dall'Olio, F. Ferrari, B. Monacelli, G. Pasqua, R. Scurria and G. Delle Monache (1989) "Cell suspension cultures of *Cassia didymobotria*: optimization of growth and secondary metabolite production by application of the orthogonal design method" in *J. Plant Physiol*. no. 135, p 290-294.

Bourgin, J.P and J.P. Nitsch (1967) "Production of haploid *Nicotiana* from excised stamens" in *Ann. Physiol. Vég*. no. 10, p 69-81.

Chatterjee, M., G. Ghosh and P.C. Datta (1987) "Role of exogenous cholesterol on *in vitro* secondary metabolism in *Thevetia peruviana* (Pers.) Schum." in *Indian Journal of Experimental Biology*, 25, no. 3, p 204-206.

Chaturvedi, H.C., P. Misra and M. Jain (1984) "Proliferation of shoot tips and clonal multiplication of *Costus speciosus* in long term culture" in *Plant Sci. Lett*. no. 35, p 67-71.

Chaturvedi, H.C., A.K. Sharma and R.N. Prasad (1978) "Shoot apex culture of *Bouganvillea glabra* 'Magnifica'" in *HortScience* no. 13, p 36.

Chikkannaiah, P.S. and M.C. Gayatri (1974) "Organogenesis in endosperm tissue cultures of *Codiaeum variegatum* Blume" in *Current Science* no. 43, p 23-24.

Chikkannaiah, P.S., K. Nataraja and M.C. Gayatri (1976) "Response of seeds and isolated embryos of *Codiaeum variegatum in vitro*" in *Current Science* no. 45, p 196-197.

Constabel, F., S. Rambold, K.B. Chatson, W.G.M. Kurz and J.P. Kutney (1982) "Alkaloid production in *Catharanthus roseus* (L.) G. Don. VI. Variation in alkaloid spectra of cell lines derived from one single leaf" in *Plant Cell Report* no. 1, p 3-5.

Constabel, F., H. Koblitz, J.W. Kirkpatrik and S. Rambold (1980) "Fusion of cell sap vacuoles subsequent to protoplast fusion" in *Can. J. Bot*. no. 58, p 1032-1034.

Cramer, C.S. and M.P. Bridgen (1993) "*In vitro* shoot proliferation of *Mussaenda* 'Dona Luz'" in *HortScience* no. 28, p 447.

Das, P., G.R. Rout and A.B. Das (1993) "Somatic embryogenesis in callus culture of *Mussaenda erythrophylla* cvs. Queen Sirikit and Rosea" in *Plant Cell, Tissue and Organ Culture* no. 35, p 199-201.

Dasgupta, M., T.K. Pramanik, S.K. Datta (1987) "Mass propagation and genetic variability of two cardenolide plants *in vitro*" in *Acta Horticulturae* no. 208, p 263-271.

Dekkers, A.J., A.N. Rao and C.J. Goh (1991) "*In vitro* storage of multiple shoot cultures of gingers at ambient temperatures of 24-29 deg C" in *Scientia Horticulturae* no. 47, p 157-167.

Drew, R.A. (1991) "*In vitro* culture of adult and juvenile bud explants of *Passiflora* species" in *Plant Cell, Tissue and Organ Culture* 26, no. 1, p 23-27.

Evaldsson, I.E. and N.T. Welander (1985) "The effects of medium composition on *in vitro* propagation and in vivo growth of *Cordyline terminalis* cv. Atoom" in *Journal of Horticultural Science* 60, no. 4, p 525-530.

Finnie, J.F. and J. van Staden (1986) "*In vitro* culture of *Anthurium andreanum*" in *South African Journal of Botany* 52, no. 4, p 343-346.

Finnie, J.F. and J. van Staden (1989) "*In vitro* propagation of *Sandersonia* and *Gloriosa*" in *Plant Cell, Tissue and Organ Culture* no. 19, p 151-158.

Foja Singh (1991) "Micropropagation and plant conformity in *Anthurium andreanum*" in Proceedings of the International Seminar on New Frontiers in Horticulture, organized by Indo-American Hybrid Seeds, Bangalore, India, 25-28 Nov. 1990 (edited by J. Prakash and R.L.M. Pierik), Kluwer Academic Publishers 1991. *Current plant science and biotechnology in agriculture* no. 12, p 201-204.

Geier, T., A. Beck and W. Preil (1992) "High uniformity of plants regenerated from cytogenetically variable embryogenic suspension cultures of poinsettia (*Euphorbia pulcherrima* Willd. ex Klotzsch)" in *Plant Cell Reports* 11, no. 3, p 150-154.

Gresshoff, P.M. and C.H. Doy (1972) "Development and differentiation of haploid *Lycopersicon esculentum* (Tomato)" in *Planta* no. 107, p 161-170.

Halder, T. and V.N. Gadgil (1982) "Morphogenesis in some plant species of the family *Cucurbitaceae*" in Rao, A.N. (ed.) 1982, *Tissue Culture of Economically Important Plants*, Proc. of Int. Symp. Singapore 1981, COSTED and ANBS, p 98-103.

Hall, T.R.H. and H.A. Collin (1975) "Initiation and growth of tissue culture of *Theobroma cacao*" in *Ann. Bot.* no. 39, p 555-570.

Halperin, W. (1966) "Alternative morphogenetic events in cell suspensions" in *Am. J. Bot.* no. 53, p 443-453.

Hegarty, P.K., N.J. Smart, A.H. Scragg and M.W. Fowler (1986) "The aeration of *Catharanthus roseus* L.G.D. on suspension cultures in airlift bioreactor: the inhibitory effect at high aeration rates on culture growth" in *J. Exp. Bot.* no. 37, p 1911-1920.

Hosoki, T. and T. Asahira (1980) "*In vitro* propagation of Bromeliads in liquid culture" in *HortScience* no. 15, p 603-604.

Jain, M. and H.C. Chaturvedi (1985) "Caulogenesis in rhizome callus of *Costus speciosus*" in *Planta Medica* no. 5, p 462-463.

Johri, B.M. and Bajaj (1962) "Behaviour of mature embryo of *Dendrophtoe falcata* (L.f.) Ettings *in vitro*" in *Nature* no. 193, p 194-195.

Johri, B.M. and S.S. Bhojwani (1965) "Growth responses of mature endosperm in cultures" in *Nature* no. 208, p 1345-1347.

Jhori, B.M. and P.S. Srivastava (1973) "Morphogenesis in endosperm cultures" in *Z. Pflanzenphysiol*. no. 70, p 285-304.

Jones, J.B. and T. Murashige (1974) "Tissue culture propagation of *Aechmea fasciata* Baker and other bromeliads" in *Comb. Proc. Int. Plant Prop. Soc.* no. 24, p117-126.

Knop, W. (1865) "Quantitative Untersuchungen über die Ernahrungsprozesse der Pflanzen" in *Landwirtsch. Vers. Stn*. No. 7, p 93-107.

Kreis, W., U. May and E. Reinhard (1986) "UDP-glucose: digitoxin 16'-O-glucosyltransferase from suspension-cultured *Digitalis lanata* cells" in *Plant Cell Reports* 5, no. 6, p 442-445.

Kuehnle, A., F.C. Chen and N. Sugii (1992) "Somatic embryogenesis and plant regeneration in *Anthurium andraeanum* hybrids" in *Plant Cell Reports* 11, no. 9, p 438-442.

Kuehnle, A.R. and G.L. Nan (1991) "Isolation and culture of protoplasts from two tropical monocots, *Anthurium* and *Dendrobium* orchid" (Abstract), Eighth international protoplast symposium, in *Physiologia Plantarum*, 82, no. 1, p A7.

Kuehnle, A.R. and N. Sugii (1991) "Callus induction and plantlet regeneration in tissue cultures of Hawaiian anthuriums" in *HortScience* 26, no. 7, p 919-921.

Kunisaki, J.T. (1975) "*In vitro* propagation of *Cordyline terminalis* L. Kunth" in *HortScience* no. 10, p 601-602.

Kunisaki, J.T. (1980) "*In vitro* propagation of *Anthurium andreanum* Lind." *HortScience* no. 15, p 508-509.

Li, Z.S., J. Attias and B. Marin (1992) "Estimation of the nucleotide pools of plant cells by high performance liquid chromatography: effect of column temperature and elution pH" in *Comptes Rendus de l'Academie des Sciences*, Series 3, 315, no. 3, p 127-132.

Lightbourn, G.J., P.V.D. Prasad (1990) "*In vitro* techniques for rapid multiplication of four varieties of *Anthurium andraeanum* in Jamaica", XXXVI Annual meeting, Kingston, Jamaica, 27 April-3 May 1990, in *Jamaica Proceedings of the Interamerican Society for Tropical Horticulture* no. 34, p 3-5.

Maene, L.J. and P.C. Debergh (1987) "Optimalisation of the transfer of tissue cultured shoots to *in vivo* conditions" in *Acta Horticulturae* no. 212, Vol. I., p 335-348.

Malho, R. and M.S.S. Pais (1992) "Kinetics and hydrodynamics of *Agapanthus umbellatus* pollen-tube growth: a structural and stereological study" in *Sexual Plant Reproduction* 5, no. 3, p 163-168.

Mathur, J. and S. Makunthakumar (1992) "Micropropagation of *Bauhinia variegata* and *Parkinsonia aculeata* from nodal explants of mature trees" in *Plant Cell, Tissue and Organ Culture* no. 28, p 119-121.

Mee, G.W.P. (1978) "Propagation of *Cordyline terminalis* from callus culture" in *HortScience* no. 13, p 660.

Mekers, O. (1977) "*In vitro* propagation of some *Tillandsoideae* (*Bromeliaceae*)" in *Acta Hort.* no. 78, p 311-320.

Meyer, H.J. and J. van Staden (1991) "Rapid *in vitro* propagation of *Aloe barbadiensis* Mill." in *Plant Cell, Tissue and Organ Culture* no. 26, p 167-171.

Miller, L.R. and T. Murashige (1976) "Tissue culture propagation of tropical foliage plants" in *In vitro* no. 12, p 797-813.

Monache, G. delle, M.C. de Rosa, R. Scurria, B. Monacelli, G. Pasqua, G. Dall'Olio and B. Botta (1991) "Metabolites from *in vitro* cultures of *Cassia didymobotrya*" in *Phytochemistry* 30, no. 6, p 1849-1854.

Montaldi, E.R. (1972) "Kinetin induction of bud differentiation on roots of entire plants" in *Z. Pflanzenphysiol*. no. 67, p 43-44.

Morris, P. and M.W. Fowler (1981) "A new method for the production of fine plant cell suspension cultures" in *Plant Cell Tissue and Organ Culture* no. 1, p 15-24.

Murashige, T. and F. Skoog (1962) "A revised medium for rapid growth and bio-assays with tobacco tissue cultures" in *Physiol. Plant* no. 15, p 473-497.

Natali, L., I.C. Sanchez and A. Cavallini (1990) "*In vitro* culture of *Aloe barbadiensis* Mill.: micropropagation from vegetative meristems" in *Plant Cell, Tissue and Organ Culture* no. 20, p 71-74.

Nataraja, K., M.S. Chennaveeraiah and P. Girigowda (1973) "*In vitro* production of shoot buds in *Euphorbia pulcherrima*" in *Curr. Sci.* no. 42, p 577-578.

Nathan, M.J., C.J. Goh, P.P. Kumar (1992) "*In vitro* propagation of *Heliconia psittacorum* by bud culture" in *HortScience 27*, no. 5, p 450-452.

Nathan, M.J., P.P. Kumar, G.J. Goh (1993) "High frequency plant regeneration in *Heliconia psittacorum* L." in *Plant Science (Limerick)*, 90, no. 1, p 63-71.

Nitsch, C. and J.P. Nitsch (1967a) "The induction of flowering *in vitro* in stem segments of *Plumbago indica* L. II. The production of vegetative buds" in *Planta* no. 72 , p 355-370.

Nitsch, C. and J.P. Nitsch (1967b) "The induction of flowering *in vitro* in stem segments of *Plumbago indica* L. II. The production of reproductive buds" in *Planta* no. 72 , p 371-384.

Nitsch, C. (1968) "Induction *in vitro* de la floraison chez une plante de jour courts: *Plumbago indica* L." in *Ann. Sci. Nat. Bot.*, Paris, 12th Series, no. 9, p 1-91.

Nitsch, J.P. and C. Nitsch (1965) "Néoformation de fleurs *in vitro* chez une espèce de jour courts: *Plumbago indica* L." in *Ann. Phys. Vég.* no. 7, p 251-256.

Nitsch, J.P., C. Nitsch, L.M.E. Rossini and D. Bui Dng Ha (1967) "The role of adenine in bud differentiation" in *Phytomorph.* no. 17, p 446-453.

Nitsch, J.P. (1965) "Deux espèces photopériodique de jour courts: *Plumbago indica* L. et *P. zeylanica* L." in *Bull. Soc. Bot.*, France, no. 112, p 517-522.

Paek, K.Y., M.O. Oh and J.K. Choi (1985) "Mass propagation of *Cordyline* and *Scindapsus in vitro*" in *Journal of the Korean Society for Horticultural Science* 26, no. 1, p 83-92. (In Korean; summary in English.)

Pal, A. and A. Roy (1991a) "Propagation of *Costus speciosus* (Koen.) Sm. through *in vitro* rhizome production" in *Plant Cell Reports* 10, no. 10, p 525-528.

Pal, A. and A. Roy (1991b) "Embryo culture of *Costus speciosus* (Koen.) Sm. to regenerate variable diosgenin yielding clones" in *Plant Cell Reports* 10, no. 11, p 565-568.

Panda, N., B.K. Debata and P. Das (1989) "*In vitro* regeneration of *Mussaenda erythrophylla* cvs. 'Queen Sirikit' and 'Rosea' from callus cultures" in *Orissa Journal of Horticulture* 17, nos 1-2, p 18-22.

Pierik, R.L.M. (1975) "Callus multiplication of *Anthurium andreanum* Lind. in liquid media" in *Neth J. Agric. Sci.* no. 23, p 299-302.

Pierik, R.L.M., H.H.M. Steegmans and J. Hendriks (1984) "The influence of naphtaleneacetic acid on the growth of *in vitro* cultivated seedlings of *Bromeliaceae*" in *Scientia Hort.* no. 24, p 193-199.

Pierik, R.L.M., H.H.M. Steegmans and J.A.J. Van der Meys (1974) "Plantlet formation in callus tissues of *Anthurium andreanum* Lind." in *Scientia Horticolturae* no. 2, p 193-198.

Prabhundesai, V. and S. Narayanaswamy (1974) "Organogenesis in tissue cultures of certain asclepiads" in *Z. Pflanzenphysiology* no. 71, p 181-185.

Pramanik, T.K., S.K. Datta (1986) "Plant regeneration and ploidy variation in culture derived plants of *Asclepias curassavica* L." in *Plant Cell Reports* 5, no. 3, p 219-222.

Preil, W., P. Florek, U. Wix and A. Beck (1988) "Towards mass propagation by use of bioreactors", International symposium on propagation of ornamental plants, Geisenheim, German Federal Republic, 23-29 Aug. 1987, in *Acta Horticulturae* no. 226, Vol. I, p 99-106.

Rahman, S.M., M. Hossain, B.K. Biswas, O.I. Joarder and R. Islam (1993) "Micropropagation of *Caesalpinia pulcherrima* through nodal bud culture of mature tree" in *Plant Cell, Tissue and Organ Culture* 32, no. 3, p 363-365.

Ramawat, K.G., R. Raj Bhansali and H.C. Harya (1978) "Shoot formation in *Catharanthus roseus* L. Don callus cultures" in *Current Science* no. 47, p 93-94.

Ranga Swamy, N.S. (1961) "Experimental studies on female reproductive structures of *Citrus microcarpa* Bunge" in *Phytomorph.*no. 11, p 109-207.

Renaudin, J.P. (1981) "Taberanthine by cell suspension cultures of *Catharanthus roseus* L.G.Don and Acer *pseudoplatanus* L." in *Plant Science Letter* no. 22, p 59-70

Ringe, F. and J.P. Nitsch (1968) "Conditions leading to flower formation on excised Begonia fragments cultured *in vitro*" in *Plant Cell Physiol*. no. 9, p 639-652.

Robbertse, P.J., J.J. Lock, E. Stoffberg and L.A. Coetzer (1990) "Effect of boron on directionality of pollen tube growth in *Petunia* and *Agapanthus*" in *South African Journal of Botany* 56, no. 4, p 487-492.

Roy, A.T. and D.N. De (1990) "Tissue culture and plant regeneration from immature embryo explant of *Calotropsis gigantea* (Linn.) R. Br." in *Plant Cell, Tissue and Organ Culture* no. 20, p 229-233.

Roy, S.C. and A. Sarkar (1991) "*In vitro* regeneration and micropropagation of *Aloe vera* L." in *Sc. Horticolturae* no. 47, p 107-113.

Satsangi, A. and H.Y. Mohan Ram (1965) "A continuously growing tissue from the mature endosperm of *Ricinus communis*" in Phytomorph. no. 15, p 26-30.

Schenk, R.U. and A.C. Hildebrandt (1972) "Medium and techniques for induction and growth of monocotyledonous plant cell cultures" in *Can. J. Bot*. no. 50, p 199-204.

Scorza, R. and J. Janik (1979) "Tissue culture in *Passiflora*" in *24th Ann. Cong. Am. Soc. Hort. Sci. Trop. Reg. 1976*, p 179-183.

Shah, R.R., K.V. Subbaiah and A.R. Mehta (1978) "Carbohydrate influence on polyphenol accumulation in *Cassia* and *Datura* tissues cultured *in vitro*" in *Biologia-Plantarum* (Czechoslovakia), 20, no. 1, p 5-13.

Sharma, A.K., R.N. Prasad and H.C. Chaturvedi (1981) "Clonal propagation of Bouganvillea *glabra* 'Magnifica' through shoot apex culture" in *Plant Cell, Tissue and Organ Culture* no. 1, p 33-38.

Soczek, U. and M. Hempel (1989) "Effect of cytokinins on growth and development of *Anthurium X cultorum* Birdsey shoot explants *in vitro*", Third symposium on growth regulators in ornamental horticulture, Skierniewice, Poland, 10-15 Sept. 1988, in *Acta Horticulturae* no. 251, p 249-254.

Somani, V.J., C.K. John, R.J. Thengane (1989) "*In vitro* propagation and corm formation in *Gloriosa superba* L." in *Indian Journal of Experimental Biology* 27, no. 6, p 578-579.

Srivastava, P.S. (1971) "*In vitro* induction of triploid roots and shoots from mature endosperm of *Jatropa panduraefolia*" in *Z. Pflanzenphysiol*. no. 66, p 93-96.

Srivastava, P.S. and J.M. Johri (1974) "Morphogenesis in mature endosperm cultures of *Jatropa* panduraefolia" in *Beitr. Biol. Pflanz*. no. 50, p 255-268.

Stafford, A., L. Smith and M.W. Foler (1985) "Regulation of product synthesis in cell culture of *Catharanthus roseus* (L.) G. Don. Growth related indole alkaloid accumulation in batch cultures" in *Plant Cell Tissue and Organ Culture* no. 4, p 83-94.

Stoltz, L.P. (1979) "*In vitro* propagation of *Acalipha wilkesiana* (Copperleaf)" in *HortScience* no. 14, p 702-703.

Stimart, D.P. and J.F. Harbage (1989) "Shoot proliferation and rooting *in vitro* of *Liatris spicata*" in *HortScience* 24, no. 5, p 835-836.

Sujatha, M. and Mukta Dhingra (1993) "Rapid plant regeneration from various explants of *Jatropa* integerrima" in *Plant Cell, Tissue and Organ Culture* no. 35, p 293-296.

Tombolato, A.F.C., S.S.G. Takebayashi, A.M.M. Costa and E. Quirino (1991) "*In vitro* culture of bromeliads" in *Brazil Agronomico* 43, nos 2-3, p 77-78.

Welander, T. (1988) "Micropropagation of *Cordyline terminalis* cv. Atoom - a European cooperation project" in *Sveriges Lantbruksuniversitet* no. 54, p 13

White, P.R. (1954) *The cultivation of animal and plant cell*, 1st edition, Ronald Press, New York.

Zhang, B., L.P. Stoltz and J.C. Snyder (1987) "*In vitro* propagation of *Euphorbia fulgens*" in *HortScience* 22, no. 3, p 486-468.

Zhang, B. and L.P. Stoltz (1989a) "Acclimatization systems for *Euphorbia fulgens* microcuttings" in *HortScience* 24, no. 6, p 1025-1026.

Zhang, B. and L.P. Stoltz (1989b) "Shoot proliferation of *Euphorbia fulgens in vitro* affected by medium components" in *HortScience* 24, no. 3, p 503-504.

Zimmer, K. and W. Pieper (1976) "Methods and problems of clonal propagation of bromeliads *in vitro*" in *Acta Horticolturae* no. 64, p 25-29.

Ziv, M. and A.H. Halevy (1983) "Control of oxidative browning and *in vitro* propagation of *Strelitzia reginae*" in *HortScience* no. 18, p 434-436.

Ziv, M., T. Yogev and O. Krebs (1986) "Effects of paclobutrazol and chlormequat on growth pattern and shoot proliferation of normal and variant *Aechmea fasciata* Baker plants regenerated *in vitro*" in *Israel Journal of Botany* 35, nos 3-4, p 175-182.

FAO TECHNICAL PAPERS

FAO PLANT PRODUCTION AND PROTECTION PAPERS

1 Horticulture: a select bibliography, 1976 (E)
2 Cotton specialists and research institutions in selected countries, 1976 (E)
3 Food legumes: distribution, adaptability and biology of yield, 1977 (E F S)
4 Soybean production in the tropics, 1977 (C E F S)
4 Rev.1 Soybean production in the tropics (first revision), 1982 (E)
5 Les systèmes pastoraux sahéliens, 1977 (F)
6 Pest resistance to pesticides and crop loss assessment – Vol. 1, 1977 (E F S)
6/2 Pest resistance to pesticides and crop loss assessment – Vol. 2, 1979 (E F S)
6/3 Pest resistance to pesticides and crop loss assessment – Vol. 3, 1981 (E F S)
7 Rodent pest biology and control – Bibliography 1970-74, 1977 (E)
8 Tropical pasture seed production, 1979 (E F** S**)
9 Food legume crops: improvement and production, 1977 (E)
10 Pesticide residues in food, 1977 – Report, 1978 (E F S)
10 Rev. Pesticide residues in food 1977 – Report, 1978 (E)
10 Sup. Pesticide residues in food 1977 – Evaluations, 1978 (E)
11 Pesticide residues in food 1965-78 – Index and summary, 1978 (E F S)
12 Crop calendars, 1978 (E/F/S)
13 The use of FAO specifications for plant protection products, 1979 (E F S)
14 Guidelines for integrated control of rice insect pests, 1979 (Ar C E F S)
15 Pesticide residues in food 1978 – Report, 1979 (E F S)
15 Sup. Pesticide residues in food 1978 – Evaluations, 1979 (E)
16 Rodenticides: analyses, specifications, formulations, 1979 (E F S)
17 Agrometeorological crop monitoring and forecasting, 1979 (C E F S)
18 Guidelines for integrated control of maize pests, 1979 (C E)
19 Elements of integrated control of sorghum pests, 1979 (E F S)
20 Pesticide residues in food 1979 – Report, 1980 (E F S)
20 Sup. Pesticide residues in food 1979 – Evaluations, 1980 (E)
21 Recommended methods for measurement of pest resistance to pesticides, 1980 (E F)
22 China: multiple cropping and related crop production technology, 1980 (E)
23 China: development of olive production, 1980 (E)
24/1 Improvement and production of maize, sorghum and millet – Vol. 1. General principles, 1980 (E F)
24/2 Improvement and production of maize, sorghum and millet – Vol. 2. Breeding, agronomy and seed production, 1980 (E F)
25 *Prosopis tamarugo:* fodder tree for arid zones, 1981 (E F S)
26 Pesticide residues in food 1980 – Report, 1981 (E F S)
26 Sup. Pesticide residues in food 1980 – Evaluations, 1981 (E)
27 Small-scale cash crop farming in South Asia, 1981 (E)
28 Second expert consultation on environmental criteria for registration of pesticides, 1981 (E F S)
29 Sesame: status and improvement, 1981 (E)
30 Palm tissue culture, 1981 (C E)
31 An eco-climatic classification of intertropical Africa, 1981 (E)
32 Weeds in tropical crops: selected abstracts, 1981 (E)
32 Sup.1 Weeds in tropical crops: review of abstracts, 1982 (E)
33 Plant collecting and herbarium development, 1981 (E)
34 Improvement of nutritional quality of food crops, 1981 (C E)
35 Date production and protection, 1982 (Ar E)
36 El cultivo y la utilización del tarwi – *Lupinus mutabilis* Sweet, 1982 (S)
37 Pesticide residues in food 1981 – Report, 1982 (E F S)
38 Winged bean production in the tropics, 1982 (E)
39 Seeds, 1982 (E/F/S)
40 Rodent control in agriculture, 1982 (Ar C E F S)
41 Rice development and rainfed rice production, 1982 (E)
42 Pesticide residues in food 1981 – Evaluations, 1982 (E)
43 Manual on mushroom cultivation, 1983 (E F)
44 Improving weed management, 1984 (E F S)
45 Pocket computers in agrometeorology, 1983 (E)
46 Pesticide residues in food 1982 – Report, 1983 (E F S)
47 The sago palm, 1983 (E F)
48 Guidelines for integrated control of cotton pests, 1983 (Ar E F S)
49 Pesticide residues in food 1982 – Evaluations, 1983 (E)
50 International plant quarantine treatment manual, 1983 (C E)
51 Handbook on jute, 1983 (E)
52 The palmyrah palm: potential and perspectives, 1983 (E)
53/1 Selected medicinal plants, 1983 (E)
54 Manual of fumigation for insect control, 1984 (C E F S)
55 Breeding for durable disease and pest resistance, 1984 (C E)
56 Pesticide residues in food 1983 – Report, 1984 (E F S)
57 Coconut, tree of life, 1984 (E S)
58 Economic guidelines for crop pest control, 1984 (E F S)
59 Micropropagation of selected rootcrops, palms, citrus and ornamental species, 1984 (E)
60 Minimum requirements for receiving and maintaining tissue culture propagating material, 1985 (E F S)
61 Pesticide residues in food 1983 – Evaluations, 1985 (E)
62 Pesticide residues in food 1984 – Report, 1985 (E F S)
63 Manual of pest control for food security reserve grain stocks, 1985 (C E)
64 Contribution à l'écologie des aphides africains, 1985 (F)
65 Amélioration de la culture irriguée du riz des petits fermiers, 1985 (F)
66 Sesame and safflower: status and potentials, 1985 (E)
67 Pesticide residues in food 1984 – Evaluations, 1985 (E)
68 Pesticide residus in food 1985 – Report, 1986 (E F S)
69 Breeding for horizontal resistance to wheat diseases, 1986 (E)
70 Breeding for durable resistance in perennial crops, 1986 (E)

71 Technical guideline on seed potato micropropagation and multiplication, 1986 (E)
72/1 Pesticide residues in food 1985 – Evaluations – Part I: Residues, 1986 (E)
72/2 Pesticide residues in food 1985 – Evaluations – Part II: Toxicology, 1986 (E)
73 Early agrometeorological crop yield assessment, 1986 (E F S)
74 Ecology and control of perennial weeds in Latin America, 1986 (E S)
75 Technical guidelines for field variety trials, 1993 (E F S)
76 Guidelines for seed exchange and plant introduction in tropical crops, 1986 (E)
77 Pesticide residues in food 1986 – Report, 1986 (E F S)
78 Pesticide residues in food 1986 – Evaluations – Part I: Residues, 1986 (E)
78/2 Pesticide residues in food 1986 – Evaluations – Part II: Toxicology, 1987 (E)
79 Tissue culture of selected tropical fruit plants, 1987 (E)
80 Improved weed management in the Near East, 1987 (E)
81 Weed science and weed control in Southeast Asia, 1987 (E)
82 Hybrid seed production of selected cereal, oil and vegetable crops, 1987 (E)
83 Litchi cultivation, 1989 (E S)
84 Pesticide residues in food 1987 – Report, 1987 (E F S)
85 Manual on the development and use of FAO specifications for plant protection products, 1987 (E** F S)
86/1 Pesticide residues in food 1987 – Evaluations – Part I: Residues, 1988 (E)
86/2 Pesticide residues in food 1987 – Evaluations – Part II: Toxicology, 1988 (E)
87 Root and tuber crops, plantains and bananas in developing countries – challenges and opportunities, 1988 (E)
88 *Jessenia* and *Oenocarpus*: neotropical oil palms worthy of domestication, 1988 (E S)
89 Vegetable production under arid and semi-arid conditions in tropical Africa, 1988 (E F)
90 Protected cultivation in the Mediterranean climate, 1990 (E F)
91 Pastures and cattle under coconuts, 1988 (E S)
92 Pesticide residues in food 1988 – Report, 1988 (E F S)
93/1 Pesticide residues in food 1988 – Evaluations – Part I: Residues, 1988 (E)
93/2 Pesticide residues in food 1988 – Evaluations – Part II: Toxicology, 1989 (E)
94 Utilization of genetic resources: suitable approaches, agronomical evaluation and use, 1989 (E)
95 Rodent pests and their control in the Near East, 1989 (E)
96 *Striga* – Improved management in Africa, 1989 (E)
97/1 Fodders for the Near East: alfalfa, 1989 (Ar E)
97/2 Fodders for the Near East: annual medic pastures, 1989 (Ar E F)
98 An annotated bibliography on rodent research in Latin America 1960-1985, 1989 (E)
99 Pesticide residues in food 1989 – Report, 1989 (E F S)
100 Pesticide residues in food 1989 – Evaluations – Part I: Residues, 1990 (E)
100/2 Pesticide residues in food 1989 – Evaluations – Part II: Toxicology, 1990 (E)
101 Soilless culture for horticultural crop production, 1990 (E)
102 Pesticide residues in food 1990 – Report, 1990 (E F S)
103/1 Pesticide residues in food 1990 – Evaluations – Part I: Residues, 1990 (E)
104 Major weeds of the Near East, 1991 (E)
105 Fundamentos teórico-prácticos del cultivo de tejidos vegetales, 1990 (S)
106 Technical guidelines for mushroom growing in the tropics, 1990 (E)
107 *Gynandropsis gynandra* (L.) Briq. – a tropical leafy vegetable – its cultivation and utilization, 1991 (E)
108 Carambola cultivation, 1993 (E S)
109 Soil solarization, 1991 (E)
110 Potato production and consumption in developing countries, 1991 (E)
111 Pesticide residues in food 1991 – Report, 1991 (E)
112 Cocoa pest and disease management in Southeast Asia and Australasia, 1992 (E)
113/1 Pesticide residues in food 1991 – Evaluations – Part I: Residues, 1991 (E)
114 Integrated pest management for protected vegetable cultivation in the Near East, 1992 (E)
115 Olive pests and their control in the Near East, 1992 (E)
116 Pesticide residues in food 1992 – Report, 1993 (E F S)
117 Quality declared seed, 1993 (E F S)
118 Pesticide residues in food 1992 – Evaluations – Part I: Residues, 1993 (E)
119 Quarantine for seed, 1993 (E)
120 Weed management for developing countries, 1993 (E S)
121 Rambutan cultivation, 1993 (E)
122 Pesticide residues in food 1993 – Report, 1993 (E F S)
123 Rodent pest management in eastern Africa, 1994 (E)
124 Pesticide residues in food 1993 – Evaluations – Part I: Residues, 1994 (E)
125 Plant quarantine: theory and practice, 1994 (Ar)
126 Tropical root and tuber crops – Production, perspectives and future prospects, 1994 (E)
127 Pesticide residues in food 1994 – Report, 1994 (E)
128 Manual on the development and use of FAO specifications for plant protection products – Fourth edition, 1995 (E F S)
129 Mangosteen cultivation, 1995 (E)
130 Post-harvest deterioration of cassava – A biotechnology perspective, 1995 (E)
131/1 Pesticide residues in food 1994 – Evaluations – Part I: Residues, Volume 1, 1995 (E)
131/2 Pesticide residues in food 1994 – Evaluations – Part I: Residues, Volume 2, 1995 (E)
132 Agro-ecology, cultivation and uses of cactus pear, 1995 (E)
133 Pesticide residues in food 1995 – Report, 1996 (E)
134 (Number not assigned)
135 Citrus pest problems and their control in the Near East, 1996 (E)
136 El pepino dulce y su cultivo, 1996 (S)
137 Pesticide residues in food 1995 – Evaluations – Part I: Residues, 1996 (E)
138 Sunn pests and their control in the Near East, 1996 (E)
139 Weed management in rice, 1996 (E)
140 Pesticide residues in food 1996 – Report, 1997 (E)
141 Cotton pests and their control in the Near East, 1997 (E)
142 Pesticide residues in food 1996 – Evaluations – Part I: Residues, 1997 (E)

143 Management of the whitefly-virus complex, 1997 (E)
144 Plant nematode problems and their control in the Near East region, 1997 (E)
145 Pesticide residues in food 1997 – Report, 1998 (E)
146 Pesticide residues in food 1997 – Evaluations – Part I: Residues, 1998 (E)
147 Soil solarization and integrated management of soilborne pests, 1998 (E)
148 Pesticide residues in food 1998 – Report, 1999 (E)
149 Manual on the development and use of FAO specifications for plant protection products – Fifth edition, including the new procedure, 1999 (E)
150 Restoring farmers' seed systems in disaster situations, 1999 (E)
151 Seed policy and programmes for sub-Saharan Africa, 1999 (E F)
152/1 Pesticide residues in food 1998 – Evaluations – Part I: Residues, Volume 1, 1999 (E)
152/2 Pesticide residues in food 1998 – Evaluations – Part I: Residues, Volume 2, 1999 (E)
153 Pesticide residues in food 1999 – Report, 1999 (E)
154 Greenhouses and shelter structures for tropical regions, 1999 (E)
155 Vegetable seedling production manual, 1999 (E)
156 Date palm cultivation, 1999 (E)
157 Pesticide residues in food 1999 – Evaluations – Part I: Residues (E)
158 Ornamental plant propagation in the tropics, 2000 (E)

Availability: August 2000

Ar – Arabic
C – Chinese
E – English
F – French
P – Portuguese
S – Spanish
Multil – Multilingual
* Out of print
** In preparation

The FAO Technical Papers are available through the authorized FAO Sales Agents or directly from Sales and Marketing Group, FAO, Viale delle Terme di Caracalla, 00100 Rome, Italy.